Standards for Evaluation Practice

D1551395

Peter H. Rossi, *Editor*

NEW DIRECTIONS FOR PROGRAM EVALUATION
A Publication of the Evaluation Research Society
SCARVIA B. ANDERSON, *Editor-in-Chief*

Number 15, September 1982

Paperback sourcebooks in
The Jossey-Bass Higher Education and
Social and Behavioral Sciences Series

Jossey-Bass Inc., Publishers
San Francisco • Washington • London

Standards for Evaluation Practice
Number 15, September 1982
Peter H. Rossi, *Editor*

New Directions for Program Evaluation Series
A Publication of the Evaluation Research Society
Scarvia B. Anderson, *Editor-in-Chief*

New Directions for Program Evaluation (publication number
USPS 449-050) is published quarterly by Jossey-Bass Inc.,
Publishers, and is sponsored by the Evaluation Research Society.
Second-class postage rates paid at San Francisco, California,
and at additional mailing offices.

Correspondence:
Subscriptions, single-issue orders, change of address notices,
undelivered copies, and other correspondence should be sent to
New Directions Subscriptions, Jossey-Bass Inc., Publishers,
433 California Street, San Francisco, California 94104.

Editorial correspondence should be sent to the Editor-in-Chief,
Scarvia B. Anderson, Educational Testing Service, 250 Piedmont
Avenue, Suite 2020, Atlanta, Georgia 30308.

Library of Congress Catalogue Card Number LC 81-48579
International Standard Serial Number ISSN 0164-7989
International Standard Book Number ISBN 87589-917-X

Cover art by Willi Baum
Manufactured in the United States of America

Ordering Information

The paperback sourcebooks listed below are published quarterly and can be ordered either by subscription or as single copies.

Subscriptions cost $35.00 per year for institutions, agencies, and libraries. Individuals can subscribe at the special rate of $21.00 per year *if payment is by personal check.* (Note that the full rate of $35.00 applies if payment is by institutional check, even if the subscription is designated for an individual.) Standing orders are accepted.

Single copies are available at $7.95 when payment accompanies order, and *all single-copy orders under $25.00 must include payment.* (California, Washington, D.C., New Jersey, and New York residents please include appropriate sales tax.) For billed orders, cost per copy is $7.95 plus postage and handling. (Prices subject to change without notice.)

To ensure correct and prompt delivery, all orders must give either the *name of an individual* or an *official purchase order number.* Please submit your order as follows:

Subscriptions: specify series and subscription year.
Single Copies: specify sourcebook code and issue number (such as, PE8).

Mail orders for United States and Possessions, Latin America, Canada, Japan, Australia, and New Zealand to:
   Jossey-Bass Inc., Publishers
   433 California Street
   San Francisco, California 94104

Mail orders for all other parts of the world to:
   Jossey-Bass Limited
   28 Banner Street
   London EC1Y 8QE

New Directions for Program Evaluation Series
Scarvia B. Anderson, *Editor-in-Chief*

Contents

Editor's Notes

A professional association, I believe, should strive continuously to improve the quality of appropriate professional activities in order to raise the average level of performance of practitioners and to reward those who reach higher levels of quality. It may also be appropriate for a professional association to censure those whose performance falls one or more standard deviations below the mean. There are a variety of devices that professional associations use to accomplish these goals: Some simply endorse role models by electing their most distinguished members to office in the hope that rank-and-file members will emulate the notables in deportment and performance. Many associations publish professional journals that seek to instruct members in improvements in the current state of the art. Many associations have codes of ethics that prescribe proper deportment in critical roles. Others have devised standards that provide more or less specific guidance for practice. Some standards set out very specific ways of proceeding; other standards provide general admonitions to "do good." Some associations have elaborate procedures to enforce standards, with quasi-judicial bodies that adjudicate complaints made against members and that censure members who have done wrong.

In its very short life, the Evaluation Research Society (ERS) has taken many of these paths with the aim of raising the quality of program evaluation. The Standards document reproduced in this sourcebook on pages 7–19 is yet another way that the ERS has taken in order to enhance the quality of evaluation activities. In some ways, the adoption of a set of standards is a considerable achievement for so young an association. Given the diversity of its members, who are drawn from a variety of disciplines, and the diversity of their interests, which range from those of individuals who procure evaluations to those of individuals who earn their living by doing evaluations and individuals who watch from the sidelines and write commentaries upon evaluation, it is a tribute to the Standards Committee that common grounds upon which all would agree (or not disagree strongly) have been found.

Why do we need a set of standards? Is it because the state of the art is badly in need of improvement? Is it because it is simply "proper" for an association to have a set of standards? Is it because standards are a step along the road to licensing? Is it because our members need backing against those who oppose them? There are many motives that support the development of standards. Perhaps it is the additive effects of all these motives that have pushed the ERS to laying out its standards.

The mixed backgrounds and heterogeneous motives are reflected in the

1

standards themselves. As Scarvia Anderson relates, the Standards Committee had to steer its way among many opposed sets of views. Many members have very strong feelings about the relative merits of qualitative and quantitative approaches. The Standards Committee stayed out of the conflict, and the Standards are mute on this issue. Indeed, as Anderson cheerfully acknowledges, the absence of specificity in many of the Standards reflects the committee's skillful steering between opposing views.

So closely did the Standards Committee attend the views of members who are evaluators that it may have paid insufficient attention to the views of those who procure evaluations. That, at least, is the complaint of Launor Carter, who finds that much mischief in evaluation can be traced to requests for proposals (RFPs) issued by harassed and untrained civil servants. Indeed, there is no reason why evaluation-funding organizations could not abide by the Standards, although there are few standards to guide the conduct of such persons.

The Evaluation Research Society is not the only source of evaluation standards. The Joint Committee on Standards for Educational Evaluation has issued standards of its own, and the General Accounting Office (GAO) has assembled some standards to guide in the judgment of evaluations of impact. David Cordray's chapter examines the extent to which the ERS Standards overlap with those of these two bodies. Daniel Stufflebeam goes into detail about the ways in which the efforts of the Joint Committee and the Evaluation Research Society agree and disagree. It is remarkable that both Cordray and Stufflebeam find little disagreement either over topics covered or over the standards themselves. Stufflebeam shows that the Joint Committee has more standards but that there is also more redundancy, because of the document's organization. Cordray claims that the ERS covers more topics than the GAO, but mainly because the GAO standards deal only with impact assessment.

Given these comparisons, one can raise two questions: First, what can account for the convergence among these three sets of standards? Second, why has the ERS developed standards of its own when apparently similar standards already exist?

My best guess about the answer to the first question is that the standards converge because they remain on the level of considerable generality. Everyone agrees, for example, that sampling methods should be described, but whether a response rate of at least 75 percent passes minimum quality standards is another matter. In short, it is likely that the same pressures toward generality were experienced both by the ERS Standards Committee and by the Joint Committee, and as a result, the results were much the same. Disagreement apparently starts where all the standards are mute. Scarvia Anderson points to the success of the ERS Standards in avoiding conflicts between advocates of "soft" and "hard" approaches as a positive feature of the document, but there is also some loss in ecumenism — a watering down of faith and vision as well as charisma.

As to why the ERS felt compelled to issue its own standards, one can only surmise: First, both the GAO and the Joint Committee standards were designed for special restricted coverage. In contrast, ERS evaluators perform a great many kinds of evaluative activities — certainly more than simple impact assessments, the topic to which the GAO document is addressed. ERS members are also concerned with a variety of substantive fields, including not only education but also (among others) criminal justice, mental health, and welfare. A document addressed to all evaluations, regardless of their substantive content, is appropriate to ERS. Indeed, one may ask why the Joint Committee addressed itself only to educational evaluation, since the standards involved are not particular to educational evaluations. Very little would have been lost had the Joint Committee addressed itself to general standards applicable to all substantive areas. Second, there are organizational imperatives for the ERS to develop standards of its own. A mature association that wants to attract members needs to have its own journals, its own conventions, and even its own standards.

Evaluation takes place within a system of clients, contractors, and beneficiaries. Evaluation contractors are not a homogeneous group, but, rather, have their organizational roots in a variety of places — universities, large research firms, and evaluation units of large consulting and research firms whose main activities range from national defense planning to consumer preference surveys. The conduct of evaluation is affected by the context in which the evaluators operate. In addition, contracting agencies (or grant-giving agencies) can affect the conduct of evaluation both through contract or grant specifications and through their monitoring of contract or grant performance.

The ERS Standards document does not address itself sufficiently to the impact of the evaluating system on the conduct of evaluative activities. Writing from the viewpoint of an evaluation research manager within a large research organization, Launor Carter complains that the Standards do not admonish evaluation procurement personnel to be aware of how their specifications can affect the quality of the evaluation procured. Since many procurement personnel are members of the ERS, it would appear that the Standards Committee could have defined its mission so as to address this issue.

The Standards also fail to address the issue of how best to manage evaluation activities within the context of large-scale organizations. Indeed, the model of evaluation activity implicit in the Standards is that of the solo practitioner, who is in complete command of everything that he or she may do. What do we say to the evaluator whose supervisor insists that he or she do the wrong thing? Since the supervisor may also be a member of the ERS, it also seems appropriate to address management roles directly.

The potentially inhibiting roles of standards are of concern both to Richard Berk and Lee Cronbach in their chapters for this volume. Minimum standards tend to become maximum standards. Many examples bear out this generalization: For example, the reason why most housing built in the United States since the 1930s has eight-foot ceilings is said to be the Federal Housing Administration (FHA) standards that specified eight-foot ceilings as the minimum for housing that qualified for FHA mortgages. Both Cronbach and Berk worry that the ERS Standards may inhibit the creativity of methodologists and thereby slow the advance of evaluation activities toward better performance. There are many ways in which standards can inhibit creativity, but one of the best is excessive specificity. Methodological procedures change with time, and the state of the art at one time may be an anachronism at another. Methods can also be rehabilitated after a lapse of time. For example, mail and telephone interviewing went into disfavor in the 1930s after the resultant sampling biases were shown to be very large. More recently, there has been a revival of interest in these data-collection methods, since procedures to remedy these faults have been devised. A standard that singled out mail and telephone surveys as distinctly inferior data-collection methods might have been worthwhile in the 1950s, but it would prove to be inhibiting in the 1980s.

Fortunately, the ERS Standards avoid many of the potentially inhibiting effects of standards by steering away from specificity. It is still possible, as Berk shows with several contrived examples, to go wrong in translating a general standard into specific procedures, but, while this might be a danger, it is hardly a high-probability outcome. For one thing, the ERS has no method of enforcing the Standards as yet. The hypothetical trial that Berk envisages — of an evaluator who uses a regression continuity of which design Donald T. Campbell disapproves — simply is not in the cards, since there is as yet no court. More likely, it seems to me, is the case in which evaluators advocating different procedures simply cite different authorities. The diversity both within the membership of the ERS and within the evaluation literature is sure to produce widely variant interpretations of standards that dictate "appropriate procedures."

Berk suggests some specific standards, stated in the form of things that persons should report (for example, response rates) or things that persons should consider in their reports (for example, selection bias). Berk argues that standards of this sort have potential for raising the state of the art and that they are beyond the realm of controversy. Perhaps that is so. But, I can think of principled objections to most of his suggested specific standards. For example, response rates are misleading indicators of the quality of data collections, since few researchers have shown that there were many important differences between respondents and nonrespondents. In short, in the present state of the evaluation field, it is difficult to state in specific terms standards that would be accepted as obvious by an overwhelming majority of the practitioners.

Lee Cronbach's chapter echoes some of the objections that Berk offers. Cronbach is more positive about pieties as standards, however, since he, like many others, believes that the symbolism of standards maybe as important as their contents, if not more so. He also makes a number of specific criticisms: First the Standards appear to view evaluation primarily as a service to management, in line with Wholey's view of evaluation. Cronbach reminds us that there are beneficiaries involved who are not merely subjects but also program participants. There is also the elusive public interest, although Cronbach tactfully refrains from giving some guidelines on how to ascertain it. Second, he makes some very strong criticisms of the failure of the Standards to refer to construct validity and suggests that we consider adopting a standard which asks that the construct validity of measures be used in an evaluation.

Both Berk and Cronbach point out that the Standards do not emphasize sufficiently that budget and time constraints (among others) usually mean that trade-offs must be made. It may not be feasible both to have the best possible sample of potential beneficiaries and to monitor implementation closely. The evaluator typically is left with the choice of expending resources on one or the other. Suboptimal procedures in one part of the evaluation may be traded off against optimal procedures in another. The principles of trade-offs are hard to formulate. Of course, one may trade off a good sample for a good interview guide, but it is difficult to conceptualize how one would make such a decision and to state such decisions as conforming to a general rule. Nevertheless, this is a neglected concern in the Standards.

Will the Standards make any difference to the ERS? Jerry Cahn, in his chapter, which explains the legal implications of the Standards and of standard making in general, answers that the main effect of the Standards will be to involve the ERS in defining what the Standards mean in specific circumstances. As he sees it, the Standards are too general and vague to result in legal trouble; for example, they do not act in restraint of trade. Furthermore, without a procedure for enforcing the Standards or for bringing charges against those who violate them, it is unlikely that the Standards will cause specific individuals to sue the ERS. However, the fact that standards exist may mean that the ERS will be called upon from time to time to provide expert witnesses on the conduct of specific evaluations.

The chapters of commentary in this volume all agree on two things: First, the standards are general and tend to stand forthrightly for pieties. Second, this quality has both positive and negative effects. On the positive side, it means that the ERS stands for tolerance within the evaluation community, gathering unto itself all the tribes of evaluations — hard and soft, formative and

6

summative, academic and commercial — regardless of creed or discipline of origin. Another positive feature is that it does not harden evaluation practices into any one specific mode, allowing for change, innovation, and progress. On the negative side, however, it does not appear that the Standards will do much to raise the average level of evaluation practice. Everybody and every procedure can be found to be acceptable, at least in some circumstances.

Peter H. Rossi
Editor

Peter H. Rossi is professor of sociology and director of the Social and Demographic Research Institute of the University of Massachusetts. He has served as president of the American Sociological Association (1979–1980), and he was awarded ERS's Myrdal Prize for his contributions to evaluation research methods.

This chapter contains the ERS Standards, as adopted by
the ERS Council.

Evaluation Research Society Standards for Program Evaluation

ERS Standards Committee

The Evaluation Research Society was established in 1976 to serve the professional needs of the growing number of people engaged in program evaluation. More often than not, evaluators work under some other official title, such as program analyst, research associate, auditor, or program planner. The programs they examine range over a wide spectrum; for example, health, education, welfare, law enforcement, public safety, rehabilitation, urban development, defense, environmental protection, training, certification, licensing, business and personnel systems, museums, and media. Further, evaluators have diverse backgrounds and come from a variety of disciplines, including economics, psychology, sociology, public policy, operations research, engineering, systems analysis, and biometry.

This diversity is reflected in the membership of the Evaluation Research Society (ERS) and is its distinctive characteristic. Recently, there was a further enrichment of this diversity of individuals and interests, which resulted from the merger of the Council for Applied Social Research (CASR) with the ERS. There are, of course, other groups that focus on evaluation within more narrowly defined domains—for example, higher education or public policy.

P. Rossi (Ed.). *New Directions for Program Evaluation: Standards for Evaluation Practice,* no. 15.
San Francisco: Jossey-Bass, September 1982.

Why Did the ERS Develop Standards for Program Evaluation?

The ERS believes that even though evaluators have different titles, work in different areas, and come from different backgrounds, they have common concerns and interests; and that evaluation theory and practice will benefit from interdisciplinary sharing. These beliefs have led to a search for standards to guide program evaluation practice and to focus attention on issues facing the emerging profession.

Some have asked why, in the face of a well-conceived and well-publicized national effort to develop program evaluation standards (that is, the Joint Committee on Standards for Educational Evaluation, Daniel L. Stufflebeam, chair), the ERS undertook a parallel activity. First, the Joint Committee's standards focus only on educational programs and would therefore not represent the broader interests of the ERS membership. Further, standards and guidelines were available from a number of other sources, including the U.S. General Accounting Office (GAO) and the Office of the Auditor General of Canada. The ERS acknowledges a considerable debt to the Joint Committee and these other sources for ideas we have borrowed and incorporated in the ERS standards.

Some have asked why the ERS limited its attention to program evaluation. ERS recognizes that program evaluation is only one kind of evaluation that is important for use in decisions about individuals, institutions, and society. However, program evaluation is the enterprise in which the majority of the ERS membership is involved. In the future, the ERS may need to give similar attention to personnel evaluation, product evaluation, proposal evaluation, and other evaluation applications. However, we felt that a more modest initial standards-development effort would stand a better chance of completion and application than an attempt to encompass such a diverse range of evaluation targets. As indicated below, the ERS standards are quite broad, even within the program evaluation delimitation.

What Aspects of Program Evaluation Do These Standards Encompass?

While some people tend to think of program evaluation as a one-shot effort to determine the overall worth of a program, in fact this is only one of several general categories of evaluation. These general categories can be defined both by the purpose of the evaluation effort and by the kinds of activities that are stressed. Some of the categories are associated more with some program contexts and settings than with others, and, as a consequence, the work of some evaluators is likely to fall more in one category than in another. However, many evaluators are comfortable working in several of the categories, many evaluation efforts encompass more than one of the categories, and indeed—especially in the case of resident evaluators in an agency—evaluators are often expected to be expert in a wide range of evaluation services. The general categories are as follows:

1. *Front-end analysis (preinstallation, context, feasibility analysis).* This includes evaluation activities that take place prior to the installation of a program: to confirm, ascertain, or estimate needs (needs assessments), adequacy of conception, operational feasibility, sources of financial support, and availability of other necessary kinds of support (for example, organizational). The results should provide useful guidance for refining program plans, determining the appropriate level of implementation, or deciding whether to install the program at all).

2. *Evaluability assessment.* This includes activities undertaken to assess whether other kinds of program evaluation efforts (especially impact evaluation) should be initiated. The emergence of evaluability assessment as a legitimate and distinctive enterprise represents a growing professional concern with the costs of evaluations in relation to their benefits, as well as with identifying the general characteristics of programs (significance, scope, execution, and so forth) that facilitate or hinder formal evaluation efforts. Evaluability assessment may encompass inquiries into technical feasibility (for example, Can valid performance indicators be devised?), policy matters (for example, Do program directors understand what kinds of information the proposed evaluation would produce? Is the funding agency's interest in the program likely to be short lived?), and, of course, the characteristics of the program itself (for example, Has it in fact been installed?).

3. *Formative (developmental, process) evaluation.* This includes testing or appraising the processes of an ongoing program in order to make modifications and improvements. Activities may include analysis of management strategies and of interactions among persons involved in the program, personnel appraisal, surveys of attitudes toward the program, and observation. In some cases, formative evaluation means field-testing a program on a small scale before installing it more widely. The formative evaluator is likely to work closely together with program designers or administrators and to participate directly in decisions to make program modifications.

4. *Impact (summative, outcome, effectiveness) evaluation.* This evaluation category corresponds to one of the most common definitions of evaluation—that is, finding out how well an entire program works. The results of impact evaluation—or of *program results review* or similar terms used in some governmental settings—are intended to provide information useful in major decisions about program continuation, expansion, or reduction. The challenges for the evaluator are to find or devise appropriate indicators of impact and to

be able to attribute types and amounts of impact to the program rather than to other influences. Some knowledge or estimate of conditions before the program was applied — or of conditions in the absence of the program — is usually required. Impact evaluations differ in the degree to which the search for appropriate indicators goes beyond the stated objectives or expectations of the program formulators, directors, funders, or other sponsors of the evaluation. However, there is rather substantial agreement that the more independent the evaluator is, the more credible the results of the impact evaluation will be, so long as the expectations of people who manage, oversee, or influence the program are reflected in the evaluation. Achieving a balance among potentially conflicting criteria will be a continuing challenge.

5. *Program monitoring.* This is the least acknowledged but probably most practiced category of evaluation, putting to rest the notion that the evaluator necessarily comes in, does the job, and then gets out. From the GAO to human service agencies in states and provinces to military training installations, there are substantial requirements to monitor programs that have already been installed, sometimes long ago. These programs may or may not once have been the subject of front-end analysis, process evaluation, impact evaluation, and perhaps even secondary evaluation (see 6, below). The kinds of activities involved in these evaluations vary widely, ranging from periodic checks of compliance with policy to relatively straightforward tracking of services delivered and counting of clients. Program monitoring may include purposes or results found also under other evaluation categories; for example, it may involve serious reexamination of whether the needs the program was originally designed to serve still exist, or it may suggest system modification, updating, and revitalization.

6. *Evaluation of evaluation (secondary evaluation, metaevaluation, evaluation audit; may include utilization evaluation).* These activities are applied most frequently to impact evaluations and are stimulated by various interests, such as scholarly investigation, requirements of agencies in coordination or oversight roles, unwillingness of the evaluatee to accept the original evaluation results, or interest in the after-effects of the evaluation on the program. Evaluations of evaluations may take a variety of forms, ranging from professional critiques of evaluation reports and procedures to reanalyses of original data (sometimes with different hypotheses in mind) to collection of new information. In the case of programs that generate widespread public interest (for example, Head Start and veterans' programs), secondary evaluators may examine the results of a number of different evaluations (including evaluations of program units and components) in order to estimate overall impact. Those involved in the relatively new movement to study whether and how evaluation results are used caution that, although utilization evaluation is included here as a special kind of evaluation of evaluation, failure of utilization is not necessarily or solely a failure of evaluation.

The preceding descriptions of six general classes of program evaluation make it clear that a broad range of meaning can be attached to the statement that someone is evaluating a program. As a frame of reference for this document, the classification scheme allows for the applicability of some standards to some categories and not to others. In fact, most of the standards apply to all categories, but when a standard is particularly relevant to only some categories, that case is specifically noted.

What Are the Standards Like and How Are They Organized?

The Standards are organized into six sections: (1) Formulation and Negotiation, (2) Structure and Design, (3) Data Collection and Preparation, (4) Data Analysis and Interpretation, (5) Communication and Disclosure, and (6) Utilization. These are listed roughly in order of typical occurrence, and all six of these phases are normally included in front-end analysis, evaluability assessment, formative evaluation, impact evaluation, and program monitoring. Secondary evaluations, however, may not include any new data collection or data analysis.

Frequently, there are significant implications of the standards in one section for standards in later sections. For example, if the Formulation and Negotiation standards are followed, the evaluator should be in a much better position to meet the Structure and Design standards. Or, violations of Data Collection and Preparation standards could make it very difficult to meet Data Analysis and Interpretation standards.

The Standards themselves take the form of simple admonitory statements. It has been suggested that more detail may be needed in some of the statements and that examples of acceptable practices in different contexts might enhance their meaning. However, the drafting committee concluded that the decision to make such additions should follow identification of ambiguities encountered in attempts to use the document and that examples of acceptable practices should be derived from those experiences.

The committee wishes to underscore its view that this initial formulation of standards is just that. This document is, and should continue to be, a live one, subject to periodic reexamination and revision.

In practice, judgment about the compliance of a given evaluation with the Standards will of course require that the context of the evaluation effort be considered. Moreover, the basis for judgment should be what an informed, disinterested party would consider reasonable and appropriate in the circumstances.

These Standards are specific to program evaluation and do not encompass the full body of legal requirements, governmental regulations, and accepted norms for professional and corporate conduct to which evaluators are subject.

Formulation and Negotiation

Before an evaluation project or program is undertaken, the concerned parties should strive for a clear mutual understanding of what is to be done, how it is to be done and why, and for an appreciation of possible constraints or impediments. However, the knowledge initially available will vary widely, and the parties to the evaluation should be prepared to modify early formulations as information and circumstances change.

1. The purposes and characteristics of the program or activity to be addressed in the evaluation should be specified as precisely as possible.

2. The clients, decision makers, and potential users of the evaluation results should be identified and their information needs and expectations made clear. Where appropriate, evaluators should also help identify areas of public interest in the program.

3. The type of evaluation which is most appropriate should be identified and its objectives made clear; the range of activities to be undertaken should be specified. (See categories 1-6, Introduction).

4. An estimate of the cost of the proposed evaluation and, where appropriate, of alternatives should be provided; this estimate should be prudent, ethically responsible, and based on sound accounting principles.

5. Agreement should be reached at the outset that the evaluation is likely to produce information of sufficient value, applicability, and potential use to justify its cost.

6. The feasibility of undertaking the evaluation should be estimated either informally or through formal evaluability assessment (see page 9).

(Some of the factors to consider are the clarity of the program description and objectives; prospects for needed cooperation; the plausibility of any postulated cause-effect relationships; the availability of time, money, and expertise to carry out the evaluation; and administrative, fiscal, and legal constraints.)

7. Restrictions, if any, on access to the data and results from an evaluation should be clearly established and agreed to between the evaluator and the client at the outset.

(In some cases—for example, government-sponsored studies where freedom of information statutes apply and where it is understood that the results of evaluation studies automatically go into public domain—the right-to-know question is not negotiable. The sponsor or evaluator is obligated to point this out at the beginning. In other cases—for example, confidential studies undertaken for private individuals and organizations—the client may rightfully expect the confidentiality of the findings to be maintained.)

8. Potential conflicts of interest should be identified, and steps should be taken to avoid compromising the evaluation processes and results.

9. Respect for and protection of the rights and welfare of all parties to the evaluation should be a central consideration in the negotiation process.

10. Accountability for the technical and financial management of the evaluation once it is undertaken should be clearly defined.

11. All agreements reached in the negotiation phase should be specified in writing, including schedule, obligations and involvements of all parties to the evaluation, and policies and procedures on access to the data. When plans or conditions change, these, too, should be specified.

12. Evaluators should not accept obligations that exceed their professional qualifications or the resources available to them.

Structure and Design

The design for any evaluation cannot be conceived in a vacuum. It is necessarily influenced by logistical, ethical, political, and fiscal concerns and therefore must take these as well as methodological requirements into account. This applies to each of the six types of evaluation specified in the introduction. Some of the principal concerns that extend beyond methodological requirements and influence the design itself are embodied in standards 1, 2, 3, 6, 7, 8, and 9. Designs will vary in rigor, and not all measurements are equally objective. However, even with these broad variations, the following standards generally apply. For example, the approach to a case study is as subject to specification as the design of an experimental study; the reliability of judgments is as much at issue as the reliability of objective tests.

13. For all types of evaluations, a clear approach or design should be specified and justified as appropriate to the types of conclusions and inferences to be drawn.

14. For impact studies, the central evaluation design problem of estimating the effects of nontreatment and the choice of a particular method for accomplishing this should be fully described and justified.

15. If sampling is to be used, the details of the sampling methodology (choice of unit, method of selection, time frame, and so forth) should be described and justified, based on explicit analysis of the requirements of the evaluation, including generalization.

16. The measurement methods and instruments should be specified and described, and their reliability and validity should be estimated for the population or phenomena to be measured.

17. Justification should be provided that appropriate procedures and instruments have been specified.

18. The necessary cooperation of program staff, affected institutions, and members of the community, as well as those directly involved in the evaluation, should be planned and assurances of cooperation obtained. (See standard 11.)

Data Collection and Preparation

These standards assume that data collection is carried out within the specifications of a sound design and plan of work. (See standards 1–18.) However, at the time the data collection methods are specified, reasonable changes should be made in the design in order to accommodate the realities of the situation. During the data collection process, if logistical difficulties occur or circumstances change significantly, the design and work plan should be revised accordingly.

19. A data collection preparation plan should be developed in advance of data collection.

20. Provision should be made for the detection, reconciliation, and documentation of departures from the original design.

21. Evaluation staff should be selected, trained, and supervised to ensure competence, consistency, impartiality, and ethical practice.

22. All data collection activities should be conducted so that the rights, welfare, dignity, and worth of individuals are respected and protected.

23. The estimated validity and reliablity of data collection instruments and procedures should be verified under the prevailing circumstances of their use. (See standard 16.)

24. Analysis of the sources of error should be undertaken, and adequate provisions for quality assurance and control should be established.

25. The data collection and preparation procedures should provide safeguards so that the findings and reports are not distorted by any biases of data collectors.

26. Data collection activities should be conducted with minimum disruption to the program under study and with minimum imposition on the organizations or persons from whom data are gathered.

27. Procedures that may entail adverse effects or risks should be subjected to independent review and then used only with informed consent of the parties affected.

28. Data should be handled and stored so that release to unauthorized persons is prevented and access to individually identifying data is limited to those with a need to know. (See standard 7.)

29. Documentation should be maintained of the source, method of collection, circumstances of collection, and processes of preparation for each item of data.

30. Appropriate safeguards should be employed to ensure against irrecoverable loss of data through catastrophic events.

*Where secondary data are used, the evaluator should try to ascertain whether the processes through which the data were originally produced conform to these standards.

Data Analysis and Interpretation

The choice of analytic procedures, like the choice of data collection methods, is more or less dictated by the structure and design of the evaluation. At the data analysis stage, the evaluator no longer has much freedom to change the design and is required to temper the analyses to characteristics of the data actually collected. New methods and procedures, some detailed and rigorous, are appearing in the literature, and evaluators should be aware of these innovations and give them full consideration.

31. The analytic procedures should be matched to the purposes of the evaluation, the design, and the data collection.

32. All analytic procedures, along with their underlying assumptions and limitations, should be described explicitly, and the reasons for choosing the procedures should be clearly explained.

(The level of detail required in the descriptions will vary with the familiarity of the procedure to the primary audience.)

33. Analytic procedures should be appropriate to the properties of the measures used and to the quality and quantity of the data.

34. The units of analysis should be appropriate to the way the data were collected and the types of conclusions to be drawn.

35. Justification should be provided that the appropriate analytic procedures have been applied.

36. Documentation should be adequate to make the analyses replicable.

37. When quantitative comparisons are made, indications should be provided of both statistical and practical significance.

38. Cause-and-effect interpretations should be bolstered not only by reference to the design but also by recognition and elimination of plausible rival explanations.

39. Findings should be reported in a manner that distinguishes among objective findings, opinions, judgments, and speculation.

Communication and Disclosure

Good communication is obviously essential to a well-formulated and well-executed evaluation and to use of the results. In particular, good communication is necessary to clarify the nature of the program, the expectations for the evaluation, and even the type of evaluation required (see standards, 1, 2, and 3); to anticipate restrictions on release of results and potential conflicts of interest (see standards 7 and 8); to establish accountability for the effort (see standards 10 and 11); to secure the cooperation of parties involved in the program and the evaluation (see standards 18 and 27); and to distinguish objective findings clearly from opinion and interpretation (see standard 39). In short, communication is not to be equated solely with the final report. However, most evaluation efforts do produce certain formal reports, intermediate and final, written and oral, and there are standards these reports should meet.

40. Findings should be presented clearly, completely, and fairly. (See standard 39.)

41. Findings should be organized and stated in language understandable by decision makers and other audiences, and any recommendations should be clearly related to the findings.

42. Findings and recommendations should be presented in a framework that indicates their relative importance.

43. Assumptions should be explicitly acknowledged.

44. Limitations caused by constraints on time, resources, data availability, and so forth should be stated. (See standards 5, 6, 7, 11, and 12.)

(Suggestions should be included about those issues and questions that need further study.)

45. A complete description of how findings were derived should be accessible.

46. Persons, groups, and organizations who have contributed to the evaluation should receive feedback appropriate to their needs.

47. Disclosure should follow the legal and proprietary understandings agreed upon in advance (standard 7), with the evaluator serving as a proponent for the fullest, most open disclosure appropriate.

48. Officials authorized to release the evaluation data should be specified.

49. The finished data base and associated documentation should be organized in a manner consistent with the accessibility policies and procedures. (See standards 7, 28, 29, 32, and 36.)

Use of Results

The usual reasons for conducting an evaluation are functional ones: to help those affected determine the feasibility of undertaking the program or to assess its operation and effects. The use of evaluation results cannot be guaranteed, of course, but it will be more likely if careful attention is given to the information needs of the potential users of the results throughout all phases of the evaluation (see especially standards 2, 3, 18, 40–46.) Beyond the day-to-day processes of encouraging responsiveness to the evaluation, there are some other considerations that the evaluator needs to keep in mind.

50. Evaluation results should be made available to appropriate users before relevant decisions must be made.

51. Evaluators should try to anticipate and prevent misinterpretations and misuses of evaluative information. (The evaluator, of course, cannot be

held responsible for misuses of evaluative information. Nevertheless, follow-up contacts with users, rebuttals of misinterpretation, and promotion of an open exchange of information should be a part of the evaluator's responsibility.)

52. The evaluator should bring to the attention of decision makers and other relevant audiences suspected side effects—positive or negative—of the evaluation process.

53. Evaluators should distinguish clearly between the findings of the evaluation and any policy recommendations based on them.

(If evaluators are called upon to go beyond the findings and to make policy recommendations or if they initiate such recommendations, they must make clear the difference between such recommendations and the actual findings of the evaluation.)

54. In making recommendations about corrective courses of action, evaluators should carefully consider and indicate what is known about the probable effectiveness and costs of the recommended courses of action.

55. Evaluators should maintain a clear distinction between their role as an evaluator and any advocacy role they choose to adopt.

(Evaluators should be aware of the apparent conflict between advocating certain positions and presenting evaluation results. Evaluators may wish to take advocacy stands, but when they do they should not assume that they possess any special status or competence.)

Sources

American Personnel and Guidance Association. "Responsibilities of Users of Standardized Tests." *Guidepost,* October 5, 1978.

American Psychological Association, American Educational Research Association, National Council on Measurement in Education. *Standards for Educational and Psychological Tests.* Washington, D.C.: American Psychological Association, 1974.

Anderson, S. B., and Ball, S. "Ethical Responsibilities in Program Evaluation." In S. B. Anderson and S. Ball, *The Profession and Practice of Program Evaluation.* San Francisco: Jossey-Bass, 1978.

Auditor General of Canada. "Study in Procedures in Cost Effectiveness: Chapter 4: Measuring Efficiency and Chapter 5: Evaluating Effectiveness." In 100th Annual Report to the House of Commons (*Fiscal Year Ended March 31, 1978*). Available from Printing and Publishing, Supply and Services Canada Hull, Quebec, Canada, KIA 0S9.

Baron, J. B., and Baron, R. M. "In Search of Standards." In R. Perloff and E. Perloff (Eds.), *New Directions for Program Evaluation: Values, Ethics, and Standards in Evaluation,* no. 7. San Francisco: Jossey-Bass, 1980.

Code of Federal Regulations. Title 45, CFR, part 46. Washington, D.C.: U.S. Department of Health, Education and Welfare, revised January 11, 1978.

Committee on Evaluation Research, Social Science Research Council. *Audits and Social Experiments: A Report Prepared for the U.S. General Accounting Office.* Washington, D.C.: U.S. General Accounting Office, 1978.

Comptroller General of the United States. *Assessing Social Programs Impact Evaluations: A Checklist Approach* (Exposure Draft). Washington, D.C.: U.S. General Accounting Office, 1978.

Comptroller General of the United States. *Evaluation and Analysis to Support Decision Making.* Washington, D.C.: U.S. General Accounting Office, 1976.

Comptroller General of the United States. *Federal Program Evaluation: Status and Issues.* Washington, D.C.: U.S Government Printing Office, 1978.

Comptroller General of the United States. *Finding Out How Programs Are Working: Suggestions for Congressional Oversight.* Washington, D.C.: U.S. General Accounting Office, 1977.

Comptroller General of the United States. *Guidelines for Model Evaluation* (Exposure Draft). Washington, D.C.: U.S. General Accounting Office, 1979.

Comptroller General of the United States. *Standards for Audit of Governmental Organizations, Programs, Activities, and Functions.* Washington, D.C.: U.S. Government Printing Office, 1972.

Division of Industrial–Organizational Psychology, American Psychological Association. *Principles for the Validation and Use of Personnel Selection Procedures.* Dayton, Ohio: Industrial–Organizational Psychologist, 1975.

Educational Testing Service. *Principles, Policies, and Procedural Guidelines Regarding ETS Products and Services.* Princeton, N.J.: Educational Testing Service, 1979.

Emrich, R. L. *Proposed Evaluation Guidelines and Standards.* Sacramento: California Council on Criminal Justice, 1973.

Emrich, R. L. *Standards for Metaevaluation.* (Preliminary version.) Hackensack, N.J.: NCCD Research Center, 1974.

Flaherty, D. H. "The Bellagio Conference on Privacy, Confidentiality, and the Use of Government Microdata." In R. F. Boruch (Ed.), *New Directions for Program Evaluation: Secondary Analysis,* no. 4. San Francisco: Jossey-Bass, 1978.

Gibbs, L. E. "A Code of Ethics for Evaluators? Detailed Responses to Questions 1 and 3 Appearing in *Evaluation.*" Unpublished manuscript, 1977.

International Personnel Management Association Assessment Council. *Standards for Item Bank Sharing.* Washington, D.C.: International Personnel Management Association, 1978.

Joint Commission on Accreditation of Hospitals. "The Balanced Service System." In *Principles for Accreditation of Community Mental Health Programs.* Chicago: Joint Commission on Accreditation of Hospitals, 1976.

Joint Committee on Standards for Educational Evaluation. *Standards for Evaluation of Educational Programs, Projects, and Materials* (Draft). Kalamazoo: Western Michigan University Research Center, 1979.

Joint Dissemination Review Panel. *Ideabook.* Washington, D.C.: U.S. Department of Health, Education and Welfare, 1977.

Klein, S. *Ethics for R&D Management: What Is Needed?* Washington, D.C.: National Institute of Education, U.S. Department of Health, Education and Welfare, 1977.

McClintock, C. C. "Issues in Establishing and Enforcing Professional Research Ethics and Standards." *Advances in Consumer Research,* 1977, *4,* 258-261.

Molner, S. F. "Trapped Bedfellows: A Comment on Windle and Neigher." *Evaluation and Program Planning,* 1978, *1,* 109-112.

Robbin, A. "Ethical Standards and Data Archives." In R. F. Boruch (Ed.), *New Directions for Program Evaluation: Secondary Analysis,* no. 4. San Francisco: Jossey-Bass, 1978.

Sheinfeld, S. N. "The Evaluation Profession in Pursuit of Value." *Evaluation and Program Planning,* 1978, *1* (2), 113-115.

Sieber, J. E., and Sanders, N. "Ethical Problems in Program Evaluation: Roles, Not Models." *Evaluation and Program Planning,* 1978, *1* (2), 117-120.

Stockton, R. *Principles and Practice for Education R&D Management with Ethical Considerations.* (Outline for a monograph.) Washington, D.C.: American Educational Research Association, Special Interest Group on Research Management, November 1978.

Task Force on Development of Assessment Center Standards. "Standards and Ethical Considerations for Assessment Center Operations." In J. L. Moses and W. C. Byham (Eds.), *Applying the Assessment Center Method.* New York: Pergamon Press, 1977.

Windle, C., and Neigher, W. "Ethical Problems in Program Evaluation: Advice for Trapped Evaluators." *Evaluation and Program Planning,* 1978, *1* (2), 97–108.

Members of Drafting Committee

Scarvia B. Anderson (Chair to 1980)
Educational Testing Service

Larry A. Braskamp
University of Illinois

Wallace M. Cohen
U.S. General Accounting Office

John W. Evans
Educational Testing Service
(formerly with U.S. Department of Education)

Alan Gilmore
Office of Auditor General of Canada

Keith E. Marvin (Chair 1980 to present)
U.S. General Accounting Office

Virginia C. Shipman
Educational Testing Service

James J. Vanecko
Peter Merrill Associates, Boston
(formerly with U.S. Department of Education)

Ronald J. Wooldridge
New York State Office of Mental Health
(formerly with Georgia Department of Human Resources)

*Over the course of several years, the ERS Standards Committee
debated the need for standards for program evaluation,
discussed and drafted standards, revised the content of each,
and finally delivered the document published here.
The task was not always easy.*

How the Committee
Built the Standards

Scarvia B. Anderson

When social scientists look over a piece of work that they have done, their tendency is to romanticize it, to remember it as it might have progressed in an
ideal unfolding rather than the way it really was. I would run that danger here if
I allowed myself an unaided reconstruction of the ERS Standards development.
Instead, I shall rely on my files and strive for some kind of narrative truth.

On July 23, 1977, the late Marcia Guttentag, founding mother of the
Evaluation Research Society, wrote: "By now, the good work of the Constitution Committee is nearly over. I am, therefore, writing to ask whether you
would be willing to take on another important task for the Evaluation Research Society. Several government agencies have been in touch with the
Evaluation Research Society to find out whether the Society would be willing
to work with them on the development of evaluation standards. . . . There is
also work currently supported by the Lilly Foundation on the development of
standards in educational evaluation. Certainly, the Evaluation Research Society should respond to these documents. Scarvia, you are. . . qualified to chair a
task force on evaluation standards. . . . I hope you will be willing to do so."

I must have said yes, because on September 4 she wrote: "Delighted
that it is possible for you to chair the Task Force on Evaluation Standards. . . .
A committee of six to eight members might be a workable size initially. Hope-

P. Rossi (Ed.). *New Directions for Program Evaluation: Standards for Evaluation Practice*, no. 15.
San Francisco: Jossey-Bass, September 1982.

fully, the members could cross substantive fields like education, labor, and health. It would also be good if they represented a diversity of methodological perspectives. Some names that occur to me are: Peter Rossi...Mark Thompson...Robert Schrank...."

Somehow, I did not attend the first meeting of the Evaluation Research Society's task force on standards, October 13, 1977, in Washington, D.C. However, Joan Baron did. In her excellent notes, she defined the two charges to the task force as follows: "To discuss the question of whether the ERS should be involved in the creation of evaluation standards; and, if so, what the standards would be."

Ronald Nuttall, Bob McCargar, Clark Abt, Steven Mayer, Reuben Horlick, and others evidently discussed the following pros and cons:

Pro

- Good standards may lead to better evaluation.
- Good standards may allow the development of better theory and training in order to meet the standards.
- Standards would provide a yardstick against which funding agencies could measure proposals and evaluation products.
- Standards would help evaluators work with employers in enabling the evaluator to explain how certain compromises in the evaluation design would lead to an inferior evaluation.

Con

- The field is too young and standards are premature.
- There is a lack of agreement among evaluators as to what the standards should contain.
- Minimum standards might lead to inferior evaluations as evaluators strive only to meet the standards.
- Growth and development of theory and methodology might be negatively affected by standards.

Joan Baron examined some of these concerns in the article "In Search of Standards" in *New Directions for Program Evaluation* (Baron and Baron, 1980).

Attached to Joan's notes on the meeting in Washington in October 1977 was this: "This is a postscript to the enclosed letter.... I do not know if the word has reached you yet, but Marcia Guttentag died in Chicago over the weekend.... The suddenness and immensity of it all leaves me quite shaken."

The first official meeting of the Standards Committee took place in Toronto, March 29, 1978, in a borrowed suite. My assistant, Claire Coles, had prepared a working paper for discussion: "First, what areas can properly be addressed by a set of standards enunciated by the Evaluation Research Society (ERS)? Second, what are the uses to which the standards will be put? Third, how detailed should these standards be? Fourth, should standards be enforced, and, if so, how?" Wendy Abt, Joan Baron, Wally Cohen, Lois-ellin Datta, and Jack Santa-Barbara were there. Eugenie Flaherty, Tom Kiresuk (ERS Ethics Committee), Steven Mayer, Ron Perloff, and Vicki Shipman were unable to attend.

At this meeting, two parallel documents were envisioned—one directed toward the commissioner of the evaluation and the other toward the provider of evaluation services. However, the group hedged: "The possibility exists that these might be collapsed into one document." Among the issues singled out for attention were these: conditions under which an evaluation is not warranted; the costs of an evaluation as compared with its worth; essential components and desirable components of an RFP; criteria for evaluating evaluation proposals; peer and agency review processes; proposal writing, including appropriate commitment of resources, what to do if the proposer disagrees with RFP requirements, and critical ingredients of a proposal; conditions under which an RFP can be withdrawn after proposals have been received; commissioner-evaluator negotiations and contractual considerations; conditions under which it is legitimate or desirable to deviate from evaluation activities proposed and how to document deviations; evaluation efficiency; coping with interference in the evaluation; dissemination of evaluation results, including how to encourage appropriate use of evaluation results; and secondary evaluations.

The second meeting of the Standards Committee was held in Washington, D.C., on November 3, 1978. John Evans, Keith Marvin, and Vicki Shipman joined the group, as did Vivian Makosky, Larry Braskamp, Alan Gilmore, and Chuck Windle, all representing the Ethics Committee. We were finally getting down to business. Joan Baron and I had collected copies of standards and standards-related documents from a number of sources. A two-day working party was set for January 1979 in Atlanta. Working party members were those who could afford the time and fare. The ERS Standards Committee had no working capital. To counter any charge of elitism, we promised to keep in touch by mail with other interested members of the ERS and the profession.

The basic shape of the document published in this volume (pages 7–19) was struck on January 29–30, 1979: formulation and negotiation, design, data collection and preparation, data analysis and interpretation, communication and disclosure, and utilization. Most evaluations, we believed, have these elements. We also recognized at that meeting that we were concerned not only with a broad range of evaluation applications (to health, law enforcement, education, public safety, urban planning, and so on) but also with a number of different forms of evaluation (including front-end, developmental, impact, secondary, and program monitoring). Some of the issues that loomed large in the discussions were evaluator competency, the use of "canned" analysis programs, internal cost-effectiveness (including the "hidden" costs of evaluation), and disclosure in light of freedom-of-information laws. Alan Gilmore went forth to draft the standards for formulation and negotiation, John Evans for design, Ron Wooldridge for data collection and preparation, Jim Vanecko for data analysis and interpretation, Keith Marvin for communication and disclosure, and Larry Braskamp for utilization.

In the meantime, as I have said, we had assembled an extensive collection of materials prepared by government agencies, professional associations, and private groups. These were useful to us as checklists, as examples of format and wording, and so on. We were well aware of the work of the Stufflebeam committee (*Standards for Evaluation of Educational Programs, Projects, and Materials,* 1981) and sought to obtain a copy of their drafts, although we were inclined to believe that the emphasis on educational evaluation was too narrow as far as the interests of ERS members were concerned. We wrote to Dan Stufflebeam in December 1978; after explaining who we were and what we were about, we asked: "Would it be possible for you to share with us a current version of the Standards? We would be most appreciative of the courtesy."

Dan Stufflebeam responded promptly that he "would be very glad to learn about the past and projected activities of the Standards Committee of the Evaluation Research Society" and "would be very pleased to have the Evaluation Research Society Standards Committee participate in our field test activities this year. If the Committee is interested in doing that, . . . you . . . should describe the proposed use of the Standards on the compliance form, sign the form, and return it to me." According the compliance form, the Joint Committee was willing to permit limited distribution of the Standards for use in three contexts: use in graduate courses in curriculum and evaluation; in meta-evaluation (that is, in evaluating evaluations); and in reports and critiques at national meetings of professional associations when specifically authorized by the chairman of the Joint Committee. There were also six conditions of use. None of the uses corresponded directly with our interests, and we were not sure that curiosity and desire to avoid unnecessary duplication were sufficient bases for requiring the Joint Committee to hear an elaborate petition from our small working party. As a result, I am embarrassed to say, we acquired a copy by what are sometimes referred to as informal means. We were impressed with the work being done by the Joint Committee, but seeing its Standards did not change the minds of Standards Committee members that the ERS document needed to be broader. As one member said, "It doesn't matter what the content of the Joint Standards is. I can never sell standards for educational evaluation to my agency."

Members of the working party met again on April 12, 1979, in San Francisco and on May 21 in Washington, D.C. For this reason, it seems appropriate to describe us as peripatetic. We were also periphrastic, hyperbolic, tautological, and plain old sloppy. After one particularly dreary session, Ron

Wooldridge commented of his own draft: "The language is ambiguous, and the underlying model of evaluation is obscure. There are good reasons for staying 'simple,' but I feel that our final version must be grounded in a firm decision-theoretic context. With no rigor of development, there is little hope that our Standards will stand up to critical scrutiny. My own suggested standard which mentions 'accuracy' and 'impartiality' is an example of a standard that careful analysis would discredit. 'Accuracy' is desirable in the restrictive case that 'loss' is an increasing function of error, but there are real situations in which our intuitive esteem for accuracy is misleading. 'Impartiality' must also be qualifed. There are situations in which all of the better procedures are biased. We may have no alternative but to create some new language. The pedestrian terminology of our field is riddled with connotations of fallacy." He felt better the next day.

The struggle to produce specific but nonrestrictive Standards — guidance that was not also a straitjacket — can be illustrated by what happened to a couple of standards in the process. For example, this standard was proposed: "Procedures and instruments for measuring program effectiveness should reflect the state of the art and be cost justified." After some transformation, it became: "Professionally outmoded or discredited procedures and instruments should not be specified for use." In its final form, it reads: "Justification should be provided that appropriate procedures and instruments have been specified." In other words, the burden shifted from having to define "state of the art" to having to justify the particular procedures and instruments used by the particular purposes and requirements of the evaluation.

Here is another example. In its first draft, this standard read: "Accountability for the management of the evaluation and the reporting of results should be clearly defined." This became: "Accountability for the technical and financial management of the evaluation, once it is undertaken, should be clearly defined." Other aspects of accountability were then spelled out in other standards.

On November 29, 1979, a complete draft of the ERS Standards was circulated to a mail-review panel (whose members had been identified early in the process) and to past and present members of the Standards Committee, the Ethics Committee, and the ERS Council, all committee chairs, and selected other reviewers. That draft stimulated considerable interest, resulted in a number of constructive suggestions for revision, and caused the now predictable schism in our profession between soft and hard evaluators to surface. As readers are doubtless aware, *soft* connotes "subjective, softheaded, sloppy," while *hard* suggests "mechanistic, inhumane, rigid." The Standards Committee had little tolerance for namecalling and insisted that it is appropriate for most evaluations to have both hard and soft components, that evaluators engaged in informal observations need to tell program personnel what they are up to, and that evaluators who employ those rare controlled experiments need to consider the rights and welfare of the persons involved. What we most feared never happened: We feared that, to gain consensus, we would have to water down some standards to the point where they became meaningless. However, perhaps as a result of our concentration on process rather than on procedure, we believe that our Standards are fairly robust.

After the Standards were revised, they were issued as an exposure draft to all members of the Evaluation Research Society in May 1980. A revision of that draft is what appears in this volume of *New Directions for Program Evaluation*. It is important to emphasize that even this relatively formal publication does not signify that the Standards have been completed. Indeed, as the Standards themselves state, "It has been suggested that more detail may be needed in some of the statements and that examples of acceptable practices in different contexts might enhance their meaning." It was felt that such detail and examples might better follow from systematic attempts to use the document. Further, as the Standards themselves specify, they are specific to program evaluation and do not encompass all the legal and professional obligations to which we are subject as citizens and as social scientists, policy analysts, or whatever else we are. Finally, our profession is new enough that we can expect some profound changes in our areas of concern and expectations for behavior in the future.

A continuing Standards Committee of the Evaluation Research Society, now chaired by Keith Marvin, will monitor these changes and the resulting need for revision. It will also consider the legislative and legal implications of the existing document, processes of utilization and liaison, and the role of the ERS in stimulating adherence to the Standards.

References

Baron, J. B., and Baron, R. M. "In Search of Standards." In R. Perloff and E. Perloff (Eds.), *New Directions for Program Evaluation: Values, Ethics, and Standards in Evaluation*, no. 7. San Francisco: Jossey-Bass, 1980.
The Joint Committee on Standards for Educational Evaluation. *Standards for Evaluations of Educational Programs, Projects, and Materials.* New York: McGraw-Hill, 1981.

Scarvia B. Anderson is a senior vice-president of the
Educational Testing Service and editor-in-chief of
New Directions for Program Evaluation. *Before serving as president*
of the Evaluation Research Society in 1980, she chaired the
ERS Standards Committee.

*The advice offered by the ERS Standards is highly consistent
with that offered by the Joint Committee Standards;
however, the author calls into question the need for independent
standard-setting efforts and proposes that the ERS and the Joint Committee
consider merging their standard-setting programs.*

A Next Step:
Discussion to Consider
Unifying the ERS and
Joint Committee Standards

Daniel L. Stufflebeam

In inviting me to comment on the ERS Standards, Peter Rossi requested that
I do so based on my experience in helping to write the *Standards for Evaluations
of Educational Programs, Projects, and Materials* (Joint Committee on Standards
for Educational Evaluation, 1981). Accordingly, I decided to address three
questions: Are multiple sets of standards for program evaluation needed? To
what extent are the ERS and the Joint Committee Standards complementary?
How might the ERS Standards be strengthened?

My examination of the first question is directed to persons working to
professionalize evaluation, since they need to know whether the expense and
effort required to maintain multiple standard-setting efforts is justified. The
second question is assumed to be of interest to users of the ERS and Joint
Committee Standards who may desire to buttress the use of one document
with information from the other. My response to the third question is aimed at
the persons who bear responsibility for revising the ERS Standards.

As an aid to addressing these questions, I compared the ERS and Joint
Committee documents, standard by standard. For each of the fifty-five ERS

P. Rossi (Ed.). *New Directions for Program Evaluation: Standards for Evaluation Practice*, no. 15.
San Francisco: Jossey-Bass, September 1982.

standards, I searched through the 120 pages of text that contain the thirty Joint Committee standards to locate the advice that is essentially equivalent to that presented in any given ERS standard. In addition, I formulated my judgments about which of the Joint Committee's standards are applicable to each of the six groupings of the ERS Standards. I encourage the readers of this review to make their own comparisons of the ERS and Joint Committee Standards and to subject my conclusions and recommendations to independent verification.

The results of my analysis are recorded in the matrix that appears as Table 1. The column headings are the six sections of the ERS Standards, while the row headings are the descriptors of the Joint Committee's Standards. The numbers in the cells refer to the fifty-five ERS standards; their placement denotes the ERS section in which each standard is found and the Joint Committee's standard(s) that, according to my analysis, convey similar information. The asterisks (*) indicate my judgments as to which Joint Committee standards are most relevant to each of the ERS sections of standards. In addressing each of my chosen review questions, I will refer to Table 1 and to my specific reactions to particular parts of the ERS document.

Are Multiple Sets of Standards Needed?

The ERS Standards document characterizes the work of the Joint Committee on Standards for Educational Evaluation as a "well-conceived and well-publicized national effort to develop program evaluation standards," but it justifies the parallel ERS effort because "the Joint Committee's standards focus only on educational programs and would therefore not represent the broader interests of the ERS membership" (*ERS Standards for Program Evaluation,* p. 2). The Joint Committee did concentrate on evaluations in education, but this is not a sufficient basis for determining that its standards are necessarily unrepresentative of the "broader interests" of ERS members. That claim should be tested, since, if it is unsupportable, there may be no compelling reason to continue investments in two independent standard-setting efforts.

I have made such a test based on the analysis in Table 1. If the Joint Committee Standards are not representative of the interests of ERS members, I should have been able to find guidance in the ERS Standards that either is not present in, or is in conflict with, the Joint Committee's Standards. I found neither. As shown in Table 1, for every ERS standard, I found one or more Joint Committee standards that provides essentially equivalent—although usually more detailed—guidance. The language of the two documents is quite consistent; some of the ERS standards overlap substantially with Joint Committee standards (for example, ERS standard 25 and Joint Committee standard D11, and ERS standard 26 and Joint Committee standard B1).

There is some material in the Joint Committee Standards that does not appear in the ERS Standards, but I do not think it renders the Joint Committee document unrepresentative of ERS interests. The Joint Committee Standards include illustrations that pertain only to education, whereas the ERS Standards contain no illustrations. No doubt, additional illustrations crossing disciplines could be developed for each of the Joint Committee's standards if this would be desired by ERS members. Also, four of the Joint Committee's standards—Valuational Interpretation, Human Interactions, Balanced Reporting, and Context Analysis—are not treated in the ERS Standards. The advice offered by these standards is hardly restricted to education, but it would be of interest to know why it is not reflected in the ERS Standards.

On the whole, the differences between the two sets of standards, in my view, do not justify the presumed need for a continuation of independent standard-setting efforts. The two projects, however, have served a useful purpose, since they have helped persons concerned with program evaluation to check whether widely shared principles within and across disciplines could be found through independent efforts. While I see the outcomes of these two projects as highly consistent, the ERS membership should make their own test.

The ERS and Joint Committee experience is reminiscent of the history of the *Standards for Educational and Psychological Tests.* That effort began with one report by the American Psychological Association (1954) and another by the American Educational Research Association and the National Council on Measurements Used in Education (1955). These two efforts were subsequently combined, and since then the three organizations have twice issued updated standards (American Psychological Association, 1966, 1974). The unification has helped the users to avoid the confusion that is engendered by multiple sets of standards.

Based on the preceding analysis and the experience in testing as well as in other professions, such as accounting and auditing (Ridings, 1980), my belief is that the organizations concerned with issuing and promoting the use of evaluation standards in education and human services should begin formal discussions about whether and how to unify their efforts. Such a unification would avoid needless duplications and expense and would promote clarity and cooperation across disciplines.

Some conditions for the needed discussions exist. The Joint Committee has become a continuing deliberative body that includes representatives from twelve professional organizations (Joint Committee on Standards for Educational Evaluation, 1980). Its purpose is to promote high-quality evaluations through the use of professional standards. Designees of several organizations not officially represented on the Joint Committee, including the ERS, have attended the Joint Committee meetings and participated in their work. Clearly, there exist good communication and a spirit of cooperation. The Joint Com-

Table 1. A Comparison of the ERS and Joint Committee Standards

| | | | | Sections of ERS Standards[1] | | | | |
		Formulation & Negotiation	I Structure & Design	II Data Collection & Preparation	III Data Analysis & Interpretation	IV Communication & Disclosure	V Utilization	VI
U T I L I T Y	A1 Audience Identification	2	18			*		*
	A2 Evaluator Credibility	6,12		21				*
	A3 Information Scope & Selection	2	*	*		42	52	*
	A4 Valuational Interpretation		*	*	*	*		*
	A5 Report Clarity					40,41		*
	A6 Report Dissemination	*				46	50	*
	A7 Report Timeliness	*				*		*
	A8 Evaluation Impact	*				*	51,54	*
F E A S I B I L I T Y	B1 Practical Procedures	6	*	26	*			
	B2 Political Viability	6		*				*
	B3 Cost Effectiveness	4,5	*					

	Code	Standard						
PROPRIETY	C1	Formal Obligation	6,7,11 *	18 *			47,48	
	C2	Conflict of Interest	8 *					*
	C3	Full & Frank Disclosure	7 *	*			40,47 *	
	C4	Public's Right to Know	7 *	*			47 *	*
	C5	Rights of Human Subjects	9 *	*	22,27,28 *		49	
	C6	Human Interactions			*			*
	C7	Balanced Reporting		*	*	*		*
	C8	Fiscal Responsibility	10 *	*	*	*		
ACCURACY	D1	Object Identification	1,6 *	*	*	*	*	
	D2	Context Analysis	*	*	*	*	*	*
	D3	Described Purposes & Procedures	3 *	13,14,17 *	19,20 *	36 *	44,45,49 *	
	D4	Defensible Information Sources		15 *	19,29 *	*	*	
	D5	Valid Measurement		16,17 *	23 *			
	D6	Reliable Measurement		16 *	23 *			
	D7	Systematic Data Control			19,24,30 *			
	D8	Anal. of Quantitative Information		14 *		31,32,33 34,35,37 *		
	D9	Anal. of Qualitative Information		*		31,32 33,35 *		
	D10	Justified Conclusions		*	25 *	35,38,39 *	43 *	53 *
	D11	Objective Reporting		*	*	39 *	*	53,55 *

1. The numbers in the cells of the matrix refer to the 55 ERS standards.
2. The stars (*) in the cells of the matrix denote which of the 30 Joint Committee standards are most relevant to each section of ERS standards.

mittee meetings provide one forum for the proposed discussion. Others include the annual meetings of the ERS and the Evaluation Network. Also, a special "constitutional convention" involving the interested parties might be organized. Whatever the forum, the proposed discussions would no doubt benefit from the developing experience and information about the two major sets of evaluation standards that now exist.

How Complementary are the ERS and Joint Committee Documents?

As shown in Table 1, there is great—although not total—overlap in the topics covered by the two sets of standards. While the advice they offer is in substantial agreement, there are some differences that tend to make the documents complementary rather than duplicative.

As already noted, the Joint Committee included four standards that, according to my analysis, are not reflected in the ERS Standards. Since these standards have been shown through reviews, hearings, and field tests to be widely shared by persons concerned with program evaluation in education, I recommend that users of the ERS Standards at least consider whether their evaluations should meet the Joint Committee's recommendations regarding valuational interpretation, balanced reporting, human interactions, and context analysis.

Another major distinction is the depth of the two documents. The ERS document mainly includes fifty-five simple prescriptive statements with no elaboration, while each Joint Committee standard includes a rationale, definitions of key concepts, suggested procedures, pitfalls to be avoided, warnings about trade-off problems, and an illustration of use and abuse. Those users of the ERS Standards who may not be thoroughly schooled and experienced in program evaluation should find the Joint Committee Standards to be a useful supplementary document. Table 1 may provide a useful device for linking and integrating the use of the two sets of standards, especially in training settings.

A major difference affecting the use of the two sets of standards is in how they are organized. The ERS Standards are grouped by main task areas in an evaluation, while the Joint Committee standards are grouped according to four attributes of a sound evaluation. In my experience, the ERS arrangement enhances use of the Standards in planning and guiding evaluations, and it achieves a measure of parsimony, since each standard is stated only once with reference to one task area (such as Data Collection and Preparation). However, this scheme of presentation makes it difficult to see and explicate all the relevant underlying principles, which is a main strength of how the Joint Committee's Standards are organized. I believe the Joint Committee's scheme of organization is more difficult to use in planning and guiding an evaluation, since, fundamentally, it requires an examination of all thirty standards in relation to each evaluation task and since each standard contains several pages of text. However, the organization of the Joint Committee Standards enhances thorough critiques and perhaps the development of a more comprehensive set of standards. For example, Table 1 reveals that the users of the ERS Standards would consider a broader scope of criteria for guiding and examining each evaluation task if they referred to the asterisked (*) Joint Committee standards in each column than if they restricted their attention to the listed ERS standards. Overall, I see the two organizational schemes as differing in how well they serve different functions.

The Joint Committee has tried to provide its audience with the benefits of both organizational approaches by including, along with its presentation of the thirty standards, a functional table of contents, which regroups the standards according to main task areas in an evaluation, much like those used by the ERS. The result is an analysis, somewhat similar to that displayed in Table 1, which seems to help users to derive the benefits of both organizational approaches. I believe the developers of both sets of standards could profitably devote further attention to finding organizational formats which best serve various user groups.

Another notable difference between the two sets of standards concerns their presentation of supplementary material. The ERS Standards are accompanied by a brief description of six types of studies to which they apply and by a list of references used to develop the Standards. The Joint Committee Standards are introduced with a section that defines key concepts (including *evaluation* and *standard*), provides an overall rationale, identifies audiences and proposed uses of the standards, and gives an overview; the presentation of the thirty standards is followed by a historical account of the standard-setting effort, a glossary, and a citation form for recording and certifying the extent that the thirty standards were considered in an evaluation. While the Joint Committee cited only references to other standard-setting efforts, they have issued through ERIC a separate annotated bibliography (Wildemuth, 1982), which is keyed to the thirty standards. Overall, then, the users of the ERS Standards can obtain considerable supplementary information from the Joint Committee documents.

How Might the ERS Standards Be Strengthened?

I agree with the ERS position that standard setting must be ongoing and that standards must be subjected to constant review and periodic revision. For the moment, I will set aside the issue of whether the long-term development and use of independent sets of standards should be sustained and will consider how the present ERS Standards could be improved.

One area for review and possible improvement of the ERS Standards concerns coverage. As indicated by my analysis in Table 1 and by my previous comments about the relative depths of the two sets of standards, the ERS Standards, in my view, omit some key principles altogether (for example, Valuational Interpretation) and underrepresent others in relation to given evaluation asks (for example, the ERS Standards seem not to provide for "objective reporting" in relation to the Communication and Disclosure function). Also, as mentioned in the chapter on the ERS Standards, future editions will probably need to contain more in-depth information concerning the meaning and use of at least some of the standards. I believe that careful reference to the Joint Committee Standards, plus widespread reviews, public hearings, and field tests would provide useful guidance for improving both the scope and depth of the ERS Standards.

The overview of the six categories of evaluation in the introduction to the ERS Standards is a useful reminder that a broad range of evaluative activities needs to be guided and checked. However, the descriptions are somewhat confusing, and, in my view, they offer some questionable advice. The definition given for formative evaluation is too narrow, since, in addition to the functions identified for this type of evaluation in the ERS document, it encompasses goal clarification and much of what is included under front-end analysis. Better labels for category 3 would, in my view, be *process* or *implementation evaluation.* The possible implication in category 1 (front-end analysis) that needs assessment occurs only before the installation of a program should be corrected, since sometimes a needs assessment is required during implementation to ascertain whether a program is worth continuing and since an updated needs assessment is often needed in a summative evaluation to provide a basis for assessing the worth as opposed to only the merit of a program. The write-up of category 4 (impact evaluation) gives the erroneous impression that summative evaluation must consider all criteria that bear on the worth and merit of a program. A useful explanation of this notion can be found in Scriven's most recent *Thesaurus* (Scriven, 1981).

The temporal ordering of the six categories of evaluation is psychologically meaningful, but conceptually it is also a trap. By phrasing and presenting the ERS Standards in the usual sequence of steps in an evaluation, evaluators have been given a practical tool to guide their work. However, the attempt to pigeonhole standards in given task areas, while an admirable attempt at parsimony, has resulted, I believe, in a distorted view that some principles, such as audience identification and information scope and selection, do not need to be considered throughout the course of an evaluation.

Another impression fostered by the ERS Standards that needs to be changed is that it is sufficient to specify a program and information requirements from a single point of view at the outset of a study. This impression is given especially by the contents of standards 1, 2, and 3 and by the fact that the issue of object identification is treated only in the first section of the ERS Standards. It would help, I believe, to modify and expand the ERS Standards so that they emphasize the importance of considering multiple perspectives in describing the object of the evaluation and in specifying information requirements and so that they provide for periodic updated prescriptions and specifications, since the program being studied and the audiences' information needs are prone to various and often unpredictable changes over time.

Another change that I believe should be considered concerns the apparent bias in the ERS Standards toward preordinate evaluation. This bias is seen in the introduction to the section on Structure and Design, where it is noted that "the approach to a case study is as subject to specification as the design of an experimental study," and also in standard 13. In many case studies and especially in responsive evaluations, prespecification of information sources and gathering devices could cause the investigators not to detect and pursue important questions and pertinent evidence that might not have been detectable at the start of the study.

The bulk of the ERS Standards' statements provide sound advice, and they are essentially free of jargon. There are a few redundancies (for example, standards 32 and 35 could be merged with no loss), but, on the whole, the contents are parsimonious.

While the ERS Standards have been presented as a living document subject to continuing review and revision, a formal mechanism for effecting the needed ongoing communication between the writers and users of the ERS Standards apparently has yet to be established. The Joint Committee has developed a clearinghouse for ongoing exchange of information about its Standards, and a form that requests and facilitates feedback has been included at the back of the Joint Committee Standards (Joint Committee on Standards for Educational Evaluation, 1981). Through these means, the Joint Committee has received a considerable number of reactions and recommendations that will be useful in the next revision phase, and it has responded to various questions and requests for assistance concerning uses of the Joint Committee Standards. Arrangements such as the clearinghouse and the feedback form seem worthy of consideration by those responsible for sustaining the living qualities of the ERS Standards.

Conclusions

In this review of the ERS Standards from the perspective of having helped develop the Joint Committee Standards, I am aware of the difficulties involved in attempting to reach broadly based agreements about what principles should be used to guide and assess a group's evaluation work. I applaud

36

the efforts of the ERS Standards Committee in getting out the first edition of the ERS Standards, as well as their initiative in securing critiques to publish with their standards.

While I have chaired the Joint Committee on Standards for Educational Evaluation for the past six years, in this review I have spoken only for myself. From my perspective, the two major standard-setting efforts have been healthy steps toward advancing the professional practice of program evaluation. The initial products of the two efforts are substantially in agreement, so much so that I see little justification for sustaining independent efforts. Personally, I believe that the ERS and the Joint Committee can serve their constituents best by merging their activities in a unified standard-setting effort. I propose a next step—discussion of this possibility.

References

American Educational Research Association and National Council on Measurements Used in Education. *Technical Recommendations for Achievement Tests.* Washington, D.C.: National Education Association, 1955.

American Psychological Association. *Technical Recommendations for Psychological Tests and Diagnostic Techniques.* Washington, D.C.: American Psychological Association, 1954.

American Psychological Association. *Standards for Educational and Psychological Tests and Manuals.* Washington, D.C.: American Psychological Association, 1966.

American Psychological Association. *Standards for Educational and Psychological Tests.* (Rev. ed.) Washington, D.C.: American Psychological Association, 1974.

Evaluation Research Society. *Standards for Program Evaluation.* Potomac, Md.: Evaluation Research Society, 1981.

Joint Committee on Standards for Educational Evaluation. *Standards for Evaluations of Educational Programs, Projects, and Materials.* New York: McGraw-Hill, 1981.

Joint Committee on Standards for Educational Evaluation. "Principles and By-Laws." Unpublished, adopted November 21, 1980; amended January 15, 1981 and October 15, 1982. Kalamazoo: Evaluation Center, Western Michigan University, 1982.

Ridings, J. M. "Standard Setting in Accounting and Auditing: Considerations for Educational Evaluation." Unpublished doctoral dissertation, Western Michigan University, 1980.

Scriven, M. *Evaluation Thesaurus.* (3rd ed.) Inverness, Calif.: Edgepress, 1981.

Wildemuth, B. (Ed.). *Annotated Bibliography to Accompany the Standards for Evaluations of Educational Programs, Projects, and Materials.* Princeton, N.J.: ERIC Center, Educational Testing Service, 1982.

Daniel L. Stufflebeam is professor of education and director of the Evaluation Center at Western Michigan University. He chaired the Phi Delta Kappa Study Committee that issued Educational Evaluation and Decision Making *in 1971. Since 1975, he has chaired the Joint Committee on Standards for Educational Evaluation. His research and publications have been concentrated in program evaluation, and he has lectured extensively on this topic in the United States and abroad.*

In the short run, the large profit-making social science research and evaluation companies will not be much affected by the Standards for Program Evaluation, but in the long run the Standards could have considerable effect.

The Standards for Program Evaluation and the Large For-Profit Social Science Research and Evaluation Companies

Launor F. Carter

The comments that follow are concerned with how the ERS Standards for Program Evaluation may affect private, for-profit social science research and evaluation companies, such as Abt Associates, Mathematica, and the System Development Corporation.

Much of the work of these organizations is based on formal contract awards resulting from proposals in response to Requests for Proposals (RFPs). Other, sometimes larger, not-for-profit organizations, such as SRI International, Rand, Educational Testing Service, Research Triangle Institute, and the American Institutes for Research, also do the same kind of work based on contracts derived from proposals in response to RFPs. In fact, the for-profit and the not-for-profit organizations frequently compete against each other and at times enter into teams that compete against other teams made up of both types of organizations. In addition, university-based research institutes, such as the National Opinion Research Center at the University of Chicago, are involved in the same competitions. From the point of view of the work that they do, about the only distinction between these various organizations is that the

P. Rossi (Ed.). *New Directions for Program Evaluation: Standards for Evaluation Practice*, no. 15. San Francisco: Jossey-Bass, September 1982.

not-for-profit organizations more frequently make unsolicited proposals to funding agencies, such as the National Science Foundation, the National Institute of Education, and private foundations. Awards from these unsolicited proposals usually are implemented through the mechanism of a grant rather than a contract and often give more freedom in the manner in which the work can be done. Foundations usually do not give grants to for-profit organizations, and government agencies always use contracts with for-profit companies. Thus, while my comments are written from the perspective of the for-profit organizations, they are generally applicable to any organization that operates under RFP-proposal-contract mechanisms.

The organizations just mentioned all have large professional staffs with Ph.D.-level training, sizable support staffs, and computer centers. Although for reasons of special interest they sometimes undertake studies costing less than $50,000, they generally work on projects of well over that size and frequently on projects costing over a million dollars. In contrast, a large number of quite small groups are also engaged in social science research and evaluation. These groups may be composed of only one or two people, who have formed a consulting organization; still for-profit, they are not capable of performing the kinds of projects done by the large organizations. The impact of the Standards for Program Evaluation on them should differ from the impact that the Standards have on the larger organizations, since these small groups generally do not have either the technical or the financial resources to perform the work specified in large federal RFPs.

Preeminence of the RFP, the Proposal, and the Contract

Since much of the work of the large contract research organizations is in response to RFPs, one must ask how the ERS Standards will affect their work. This work is performed in accordance with fairly well-defined statements of work and conditions specified in the contract documents. RFPs often specify in considerable detail the work to be performed and how it is to be carried out. There are three ways in which the Standards for Program Evaluation could influence this work. First, the RFP itself could contain references to the Standards, stating explicitly that the work was to be done in accordance with the Standards. It is more likely, however, that the RFP will formulate the statement of work or tasks to be performed in such a way that the ideas embodied in the Standards are included implicitly in the statement of work. Note that in such instances it is the government that accepts and requires the Standards. This is the most straightforward way of assuring that the Standards have an impact and are followed.

The second way in which the Standards can influence the work is by being included in the proposal. That is, although the RFP does not include the

Standards, the proposer may incorporate them into the proposal, either in full or by having elements of the Standards written into the appropriate parts of the proposal.

Will proposers do so? If a proposer sees some advantage to including the Standards in the proposal, they will be included, but if inclusion increases the costs or is in some way not compatible with the RFP, the proposer will probably remain silent with regard to the question of the Standards. From the proposer's point of view, the primary purpose of the proposal is to win a contract. If the RFP is at least fairly reasonable regarding the work required and the amount of resources that the contract makes available, proposers will propose to do the work specified and will try to convince the government that they can do the work better than other proposers. In my long experience with RFPs, I can recall only one RFP where we refused to propose because we felt the work required was unreasonable from the standpoint of the resources available. This was a RFP for more than a million dollars: We wrote a proposal based on the original RFP, but the agency concerned later required additional work without increasing the funds available. We refused to modify our proposal, although the agency urged us to do so. The contract resulting from this RFP was awarded to a university research institute that agreed to the additional work. After less than a year, the contract was cancelled because the agency felt that the contractor was unable to perform as agreed in the modified proposal. I cite this instance to make two points. First, it is very seldom that social science research and evaluation companies do not propose on an RFP that they think they have a reasonable chance of winning. Second, since cost is such an important factor, they will not make proposals that include the Standards if they think that including the Standards will increase the costs beyond what is available. Incidentally, some RFPs ask for some of the work to be done in ways that are less than adequate or inefficient. In my experience, the proposers almost always agree to do the work in the way it is asked for, but they may also propose alternate ways that they think are preferable. Proposers need to draw a fine line regarding the degree to which they can deviate from the work required in an RFP, since they thereby run the risk of being declared nonresponsive and of having their proposal removed from competition. Thus, if the Standards are not at least acceptable to the procuring agency, they will not be included in the proposal. It is also worth pointing out that the agency that evaluates proposals is not a faceless organization. Rather, proposals are evaluated by federal employees. If the particular employees do not value the Standards, the Standards will not be used.

The third way in which ERS Standards can have an impact on the work is by being incorporated into the boiler plate of the contract. Every government contract spells out the statement of work and incorporates the proposal as a part of the contract. In addition, there are pages and pages of fine print specifying such items as government accounting standards, rights to data, ways in which payments are to be made, computer standards to be used, and other items. A simple way to include the Standards for Program Evaluation in government evaluations is to have them included in the boiler plate as a standard part of the terms and conditions. Perhaps the Evaluation Research Society could persuade the Office of Management and Budget to require that the Standards be included routinely in all government evaluation contracts. Then, all agencies would have to embrace them, and all proposers would have to follow them.

Large Evaluation Organizations and the Various Aspects of Program Evaluation

The Standards cover six different aspects of program evaluation. Large organizations have done work in all six areas, although the extent of their involvement is somewhat different from area to area. In the area of front-end analysis, it might be thought that members of congressional staffs and executive agencies would do the work to determine the need for new programs, but often the determination of need and of the feasibility of proposed programs becomes a major undertaking. Perhaps the best example of feasibility analysis done under contract is the major study of the negative income tax idea that was the subject of the Income Maintenance Experiments. The several studies (Rossi and Lyall, 1976) undertaken in this area involved a number of geographically dispersed locations in rural and urban settings. Several major research organizations both at universities and in the private sector were involved. Similarly, a major organization has been involved in assessing the feasibility of various prepaid health insurance plans.

The next area, evaluability assessment, has come to the fore in the last few years. It has been proposed that evaluability assessment should be undertaken by the government agency that has jurisdiction over the program to be assessed. But, most government agencies do not have the manpower resources to undertake such assessments, and frequently they have contracted them out. I have seen RFPs that make the study of the feasibility of an evaluation of the program one of the first steps in the work statement. I have always thought this to be a peculiar requirement, since it is hard to imagine that a contractor who has gone to the expense of writing a proposal, winning it, building up a staff and committing management resources to undertake the evaluation will ever find that the program is not capable of being evaluated.

Indeed, it is surprising how often the first step in a large evaluation contract is to do an extensive description of the program itself. The federal monitors of the program usually know how the program is supposed to work, but they freely admit that they do not know the range of variation involved in its implementation. In fact, I can think of many major evaluation efforts in which one of the most important aspects of the evaluation has been a description of the program and how it works, rather than the evaluation of its impact.

The difference between formative and summative evaluations is not as clear as people sometimes suggest. Perhaps the size and formality of the two kinds of evaluations are worthy of distinction, but from the point of view of those who perform such evaluations, it seems clear that, simply as a result of the staff required, small organizations cannot properly perform either formative or summative evaluations of large national programs. In contrast large organizations have successfully done both. The same can be said of program monitoring.

Evaluation of evaluations can be done by both large and small groups. I know of instances where large private organizations have done extensive secondary evaluations, but it seems that when a government agency sponsors a secondary analysis, it wants the prestige—and supposed impartiality— associated with universities. While I think that large private organizations are perfectly capable of undertaking secondary evaluations, I believe that usually the government agency wanting the secondary evaluation would not receive the kind of certification that it is seeking if the secondary evaluation was done by a for-profit organization.

The Standards as They Apply to Large Organizations

The Standards are organized into six areas. Initially, it should be said that the Standards are reasonable and represent desirable goals but that problems may arise in implementing some of them. Since most of the Standards are both desirable and implementable, I will only comment on those where I think there may be some difficulty in achieving the desirable end result.

Formulation and Negotiation. Standard 4 deals with the costing of proposals. It says that the costing should be prudent, ethically responsible, and based on sound accounting principles. No one can argue that this standard is desirable, but it is most difficult to know how to price a proposal prudently. Usually, each section of a proposal is written by a different staff member. Each staff member estimates the amount of staff time that will be required to accomplish the task described in the section as well as the amount of travel involved, the amount of computer time required, the cost of printing and purchasing supplies, and so on. Then, the costs of supervision and administration are determined. All these are added up with the corporate overhead rates and expected profit percentage added to obtain a final price. Usually, RFPs or contacts with the issuing agencies provide good estimates either of the costs that the agencies expect or of the amount of money that is available. Almost invariably, the first total of estimated costs is considerably higher than the amount of money available. What do you do then? You go over the cost estimates and try to cut out any fat—things that it would be nice to do but that are not absolutely essential. So, you reduce the sample size, you make fewer visits to the customer, you reduce the amount of staff time, and you do anything else that seems reasonable but still leaves enough money to do a responsible job. Usually, the costs are still somewhat too high, but you submit the proposal anyway and hope that the agency will accept it and find the money.

This is the way in which my firm normally managed the costing process. Nevertheless, I have known instances where competing organizations made winning cost proposals that were less than one half of what I thought was our rock-bottom price. Of course, these organizations have also come in for cost overruns as the work progressed. Thus, the problem of pricing has two sides: First, there is the ethical problem of proposers' deliberately undercosting. At times, we protested awards that we thought were deliberately undercosted. Once, we actually had an award overturned. By the time it was overturned, however, a year had elapsed, and the agency decided to have the low bidder continue the work, since it was near completion. All we got out of this was some moral satisfaction and the burden of bearing the costs of the appeal. In theory, the government should examine future proposals from such companies with a skeptical eye, but government agencies do not exchange much information of this sort, and their memories are only as good as the individuals involved. I doubt that the low-bidding organizations really hurt themselves much.

Second, there is the problem of the way in which the government negotiates contracts. I have taken part in contract negotiations where our cost proposal was examined in minute detail. We were required to justify each trip, to cost the per diem rate, the overhead rates, the amount of manpower proposed for each part of the work; and so on. This seemed reasonable, and, except for some odd ideas about what items like hotels cost, I appreciated such careful examination of our costs. However, I have also taken part in negotiations where no attention at all seemed to be paid to the costing—and in the same agency! The difference seemed to be made by the contract officer that we drew. To make standards work, we need responsible proposers on the one hand, but, even more important, we need careful and detailed government contract cost negotiations.

Standard 5 argues that agreement should be reached at the outset on whether the evaluation is likely to produce information of sufficient value, applicability, and potential use to justify the cost. Perhaps there may be instances where this desirable type of agreement is reached or even discussed, but in my many years of government evaluation work I can think of no instance where this issue was ever raised. If the government goes to the trouble of issuing an RFP, it is hard to imagine that a company will ask the government if it really wants to do the evaluation. I have known instances where questions have been raised about the feasibility of certain aspects of the RFP, or where alternative procedures have been proposed, or where we have not made a proposal because we thought the work could not be done in the way in which the government proposed doing it, but in the RFP situation one does not raise questions about the value of the work or about whether there is enough potential use in the work to justify its cost. Perhaps in unsolicited proposal situations or in dealing with small unsophisticated customers, such a standard may have some justification, but I doubt that it is relevant in dealing with the federal government in formal proposal situations.

Standard 6, which bears on the feasibility of an evaluation, involves some of the same difficulties as those just discussed, at least from the standpoint of the proposer. Perhaps Standard 6 has been included as an admonition to the government in issuing RFPs, but some of the items that it mentions are usually among the first steps that a contractor undertakes as a part of the evaluation. Almost always, the first step in working on an evaluation is a survey of the local organizations conducting the program to determine what the program really consists of, how it has been implemented, how it varies from site to site, and what the goals of the actual implementers are. Likewise, the contractor sees it as one of his responsibilities to achieve needed cooperation, and methods for achieving this are derived from experience and the proven techniques that are a part of the contractor's know-how. Incidentally, the payment of respondents and staff members of the organizations being studied for extra time required in the evaluation should be a standard procedure. After all, people value their own time, and we should recompense them for using that time. Clearly, the feasibility of undertaking an evaluation should be estimated — not informally, but formally through the instrument of proposals and contract or grant agreement.

Structure and Design. The standards under this heading are all clearly desirable, but the time at which they apply could be more clearly specified. Do they apply to the proposal phase, the planning phase, the analysis phase, or the writing of the technical reports? Actually, in large federal evaluation projects, considerations of design are of concern throughout the project. Usually, the RFP specifies the general character of the design. In the proposal, the design is elaborated, and problems of implementation are detailed. Usually, there is a requirement for an external research advisory committee, whose members are expected to contribute to the design. When actual implementation is attempted, various problems can arise in drawing the sample and in collecting data. These problems can influence the design and have an impact on the analysis. Finally, when the technical reports are written, their writers try to present the design both as it was conceived and as it actually was implemented. The standards on structure and design would be stronger if they considered design as it is related to the time phasing of the project.

Data Collection and Preparation. Twelve standards are devoted to data collection and preparation. It is good to see this amount of attention paid to an often neglected subject. Frequently, the largest amount of money and time required by an evaluation is spent on this phase of the work, but it is often relegated to secondary importance in favor of the more technical analytical work.

Standard 22 states "All data collection activities should be conducted so that the rights, welfare, dignity, and worth of the individuals are respected and protected." While I do not disagree with this standard, I suggest that at times we may have gone too far in the protection of the rights of individuals. For the last seven years, I have been involved in a project involving some 120,000 elementary school children. We have collected several hundred items of information on each child over a three-year period. To ensure that we never knew the name of a single child in the study, we were required to use an elaborate coding and number-matching scheme. This cost hundreds of thousands of dollars. What was the purpose? What possible harm could have come from our knowing the names of these children? It seems to me that we need to strike a better balance between the cost of preserving anonymity and the possible harmful effects of breaching anonymity. There is another area, however, where anonymity is important, and that is in retaining information about cooperating institutions so that it cannot be used to their detriment. In the case of the study just mentioned, we never reported the names of the schools involved to the government; thus, no one could obtain the information under the Freedom of Information Act, since it was not in government files.

Standard 28 emphasizes that data should be handled and stored so that release to unauthorized persons is prevented. Certainly, this is consistent with the point just made. Nevertheless, the data collected during evaluations are often a rich resource for further research, and they should be made available for secondary analysis. It is easy to prepare data tapes that identify each case by code number and omit individual names. Such data tapes can now be deposited with the National Archives, and researchers can purchase them for nominal sums. Page and Keith (1981) indicate that the data set for the High School and Beyond study is available from the Archives, and the recent Sustaining Effects Study (Carter, 1980) has been filed with the Archives. Researchers should take advantage of these rich resources, since they represent collections of data in which millions of dollars have been invested; certainly, they contain the basic data for many important additional studies.

Data Analysis and Interpretation. Again, one can applaud the standards placed under this heading and yet wish they they were somewhat more explicit as to when and where they are applicable. For example, standard 32 says, "All analytic procedures, along with their underlying assumptions and limitations, should be described explicitly, and the reasons for choosing the procedures should be clearly explained." Parenthetically, it adds "The level of detail required in the descriptions will vary with the familiarity of the procedure to the primary audience." Now, how is this standard to be applied? Certainly, if the primary audience of a report consists of other professional colleagues, one may want to justify the particular analytical procedures chosen, but it is clearly not necessary to give all the assumptions underlying them, since other analysts will be familiar with them. In contrast, if the audience for the report is largely composed of administrative and legislative staffs, then one does not want to provide a detailed rationale for the particular techniques chosen or for the assumptions underlying them, since that is the surest way to guarantee that the report will not be read. If there are questions about the appropriateness of the analyses, they should be stated in simple English, and their implications should be noted. It is difficult to determine how much technical detail should be put into a report. The trouble with such standards as these is that they are well-intentioned but not really very helpful in giving guidance to the authors of reports.

Communication and Disclosure. It goes without saying that full and open disclosure of findings and reports is desirable and should be urged by the contractor. But, at the same time, the method of reporting findings is usually clearly specified in the contract between the government and the contractor. It is usually specified that the government agency is the only one authorized to release the results of an evaluation. At times, this can be annoying to the contractor, because it often seems that the release of their reports is unnecessarily delayed. I do not believe that this delay is usually deliberate on the part of the contracting government agency, but the rules surrounding release can delay release beyond reason. Procedures differ from department to department, but a typical procedure includes the following: The report is received by the government project officer for initial review. It is reviewed and returned to the contractor with suggestions for modification. The contractor revises the report and formally submits it for release. The government project officer reviews the report and writes a short executive summary in the format required by the agency. The report, with the executive summary, is sent to the project officer's immediate superior for review. After review and possible revision, it is forwarded to the agency headquarters, where it may be subject to further suggestions regarding possible changes in the interpretation and recommendations. After it is reviewed by the agency head, it is sent to the department for review and forwarding to Congress, if it is a mandated study. Congress has sixty days to react and ask for clarification. If all goes well, the report can then be released by the contractor. I have known this process to take several years. The delay resulted not from any intention on the part of the government to suppress the report but from delay on the part of the project officer in writing the executive summary, from changes in the government personnel who were responsible, from changes in rules about the release of reports that went into effect while the report was being processed, and from simple bureaucratic inertia. It might be helpful if the Standards contained some words specifically directed to government agencies about prompt release of reports.

Use of Results. Two of the questions most frequently asked evaluators are "What did you learn?" and "What do your results indicate that we should do?" These are somewhat different questions. One asks what new knowledge was gained from the study, and the other asks what action should be taken as a result of this knowledge. Often, there is disagreement among government officials as to whether contractors should answer one or both questions in their evaluation reports.

On the one hand, some believe that the contractor should present results and that government officials should draw interpretations and recommendations. These people argue that contractors know only the results from the study, not all the policy considerations surrounding the program being evaluated. Furthermore, these people say that it is not the contractor's role to recommend policy; that is the proper role of government officials and legislators.

On the other hand, it also seems reasonable to take the position that contractors probably know more about the program being evaluated than anyone else, either inside or outside the government. Thus, contractors are in a good position to make recommendations about how the program should be changed. I tend to lean toward the latter position. While contractors certainly do not know all the concerns surrounding a particular program, they probably have acquired a better perspective during the period required for a lengthy evaluation than anyone else already possesses. If the government agency does not wish to adopt the contractor's recommendations, that is understandable, but to prohibit the contractor from making recommendations, as has been the case in some instances, is to deprive the government of the full benefit that might be derived from an evaluation. In addition, if contractors know that they will be required to make recommendations, they may well conduct the evaluation more rigorously and pragmatically.

Incidentally, I do not agree with the last sentence of the standard 55, which says "Evaluators may wish to take advocacy stands, but when they do they should not assume that they possess any special status or competence." If evaluators do take an advocacy position, they may not have any special status, but as a result of their long involvement in evaluating the program, they should surely have some special competence. Indeed, if they do not have special competence, the results of the evaluation seem almost irrelevant to the policy debate involved.

Conclusion

In the chapter on the ERS Standards, the Standards Committee says, "The Standards themselves take the form of simple admonitory statements." My *New Webster's Dictionary of the English Language* gives the meaning of *admonish* as "To warn or notify of a fault; to reprove with mildness; to advise or exhort; to recall or urge to duty." Perhaps this is as strong as we can be at this stage of the development of the evaluation profession, but most professional organizations have a code of ethics or conduct that has more teeth to it than this term evokes. Doctors and lawyers have codes that can result in their expulsion from their professional organizations and often in loss of their license to practice. The American Psychological Association has published the *Ethical Standards of Psychologists* (American Psychological Association, 1953) which was developed after collection of a large number of incidents of possible unethical actions. Based on these incidents, a number of statements were developed and categorized by areas of concern. General principles were stated, and examples of the kinds of questionable conduct were given. The bylaws of the association clearly define the procedures to be followed when a member is accused of violating one or more of the principles defined in the *Ethical Standards*. A committee of scientific and professional ethics and conduct, which I once chaired, hears complaints, gives the accused the right to be heard and to be represented by counsel, and makes recommendations to the Association's board of directors regarding expulsion of the member involved. If a member is expelled from the Association, the members of the Association are informed by a confidential memorandum. In many states, the practice of psychology is regulated or licensed, and membership in the appropriate professional organization is often a prerequisite for obtaining a license. Thus, ethical charges are serious matters that can affect the ability of a psychologist to earn a living. Also, since the matter is so serious, it behooves the Association to be particularly judicious in the case of members accused of unethical practices, not only because of fairness to the member involved but also because of the possibility of libel and other legal actions against the Association. I do not at this time advocate that the Evaluation Research Society develop standards having this degree of formality, but as experience is gained with the present Standards, we should seriously consider moving in the same direction regarding a code of conduct as other professional associations have already moved. Is program evaluation any less important than other responsible professional services, and should it be done with any less care than the members of these professions customarily display?

48

References

American Psychological Association. *Ethical Standards of Psychologists.* Washington, D.C.: American Psychological Association, 1953 (and later editions).

Carter, L. F. *The Sustaining Effects Study: An Interim Report.* Santa Monica, Calif.: System Development Corporation, 1980.

Page, E. B., and Keith, T. Z. "Effects of U.S. Private Schools: A Technical Analysis of Two Recent Claims." *Educational Researcher,* 1981, *10* (7), 7–18.

Rossi, P. H., and Lyall, K. *Reforming Public Welfare: A Critique of the Negative Income Tax Experiment.* New York: Russell Sage Foundation, 1976.

From 1955 to 1981, Launor F. Carter was with the System Development Corporation (SDC), where he served as vice-president for research and development and, from 1975 until his retirement in 1981, as vice-president for studies and evaluation. During this period, SDC performed a number of large evaluation studies for the U.S. Office of Education, the Department of Agriculture, the Department of Defense, and the state of California. Carter was director of the Sustaining Effects Study mentioned in this chapter.

*This chapter lists the potential benefits and dangers of standards
and assesses whether the ERS Standards are beneficial on balance.*

In Praise of Uncertainty

Lee J. Cronbach

Two sentiments about the ERS Standards I express at the outset. First, the document as it stands is as satisfactory as could be hoped for in this field at this time. Every principle is open to a reasonable interpretation. Second, murky depths lie beneath statements that seem like placid pools reflecting a limpid sky. Like Descartes, "I encountered nothing so dubious that I could not draw from it some conclusion that was tolerably secure, if this were no more than the inference that it contained in it nothing that was certain" (1969 [1637], p. 99).

The evaluation community will gain something if every member takes these standards as a Hippocratic oath. The community will gain a more profound education if each reader asks of each standard: Under what circumstances would it make sense to go counter to this advice? My critical remarks are intended to stimulate this instructive process, not to scorn the Standards Committee's gift.

Standards: Intentions and Side Effects

Standards have functions, intentional and unintentional. I propose to explore these functions before I consider the probable role of the evaluation standards. This is an opportunity to reflect on what has been in the back of my mind since the early 1950s, when I was one of the group appointed to formu-

P. Rossi (Ed.). *New Directions for Program Evaluation: Standards for Evaluation Practice*, no. 15.
San Francisco: Jossey-Bass, September 1982.

late what became known as the *Standards for Educational and Psychological Tests* (American Psychological Association, 1954; 1974).

By definition, the function of a standard is to standardize. But, standardization is inimical to innovation; should an agency want to standardize practice? The American Psychological Association (APA) committee that prepared the document on testing tried to avoid a standardizing effect, and so, it seems, did the ERS committee. What can be the function of standards that do not standardize? Before I speak to that point, let me consider functions of standardizing.

Some standards institutionalize mere conventions, for what must be aesthetic reasons. Excellence at the hundred-meter dash is not more meritorious than excellence at eighty-two meters. The hundred-meter standard enhances excellence, however, enabling athletes to perfect techniques specific to a distance, as they could not in preparing for races of miscellaneous lengths. A haiku of seventeen syllables is not intrinsically preferable to a poem of fifteen syllables, but poems that satisfy that additional, arbitrary specification give prouder evidence of human determination. Just as some runners are better at one distance than another, so are some talents presumably better able to express images in fifteen syllables than seventeen. Not only can standards penalize arbitrarily selected producers; as abortifacient, the seventeen-syllable standard deprives the world of delightful fifteen-syllable poems. In general, imposition of conventions supports an academic smugness that has repeatedly brought sterility to arts.

Some standards are intended to raise the quality of information and so to increase the power of purchasers, an example being the octane numbers posted on gasoline pumps. To help consumers become masters of their fate is a fine objective, but even information standards can carry a price. The variable that is standardized tends to become the mark of excellence, while other qualities tend to be overlooked. Americans came to think of automobile engines in terms of horsepower; if a standard for engine efficiency had been advertised over the decades, it would have changed the history of the industry. The old requirement that margarine be white implied its inferiority to butter and inhibited consumer choice.

Reducing cost is one motive for restricting variety. Huge inventories of replacement parts are needed if dimensions vary with the whim of their maker. It was impractical to ship goods over long distances when reloading was required because one rail line ended and the next continued on a different gauge. Paradoxically, reducing variety can increase consumers' options and expand competition. But, standards such as building codes can also keep superior technology from coming into use. Indeed, standards are typically designed to restrain trade. Certification requirements for entry into a profession are one conspicuous example. Such standards are almost never validated empirically, and they often reflect only the view predominant in a given time.

A standard is likely to be a political compromise, after hard-liners demand severe restriction, and heterodox objections cumulate in a call for laissez faire. Political forces can be so balanced, or understanding of the topic can be so immature, or the topic can be inherently so complex that the standards are no more than platitudes. Those who legislate inexplicit standards endow bureaucrats with power that can be abused. The stringency of guidelines and the rigor of enforcement can shift with the political balance.

The APA test standards were left deliberately open. Some zealots of 1950 wanted to discourage "invalid" tests and hoped to set some unequivocal standard—perhaps something like "The validity coefficient must reach 0.40 before a test is recommended for a given use." Alternative views prevailed; the standards did not draw a line between good tests and bad. Rather, they called for providing professionals with information that would enable each one to judge a test's adequacy for the use intended. Since the research to collect such information was costly, the standards discouraged development of innovative tests with small markets. Test development came to be concentrated in well-capitalized firms that sought returns by producing for the largest, hence most traditional, markets. In the 1970s, government regulations and court opinions on fair employment incorporated the standards by reference; their deliberate equivocality then proved to be an embarrassment, because employers could not demonstrate that they were in compliance.

Standards, even weak ones that do nothing to restrain practice, have a symbolic function. They are reminders of community ideals; loyalty to motherhood and apple pie contribute to social stability, even though some mothers produce indigestible pies. Also, pronouncing in favor of virtue advertises the virtue of the pronouncer. For an organization to issue a set of standards is to claim maturity of thought for the field and puberty for the group itself. Each subsequent edition reasserts a claim to authority over the territory staked out. The sheer existence of the APA test standards strengthened the influence of the psychological profession when regulatory agencies took aim at personnel testing.

The Placid Surface

It is neither surprising nor unsuitable that the ERS Standards reiterate pieties. Evaluators should be competent (standards 6, 12, and 21), respectful of those whom they observe and or sponsors (standards 9 and 22), attentive to their own biases (standards 8 and 15), and lucid about plans and findings (standards 13, 40, and 41).

The standards are delicately worded, bespeaking an admirable diplomacy that found language to accommodate many points of view. The document has an ecumenical concept of the profession; no hint appears that competence in statistics or in economics, say, counts for more than any other qualification. A crucial sentence discourages would-be enforcers from taking the Standards as literal and inviolable; in no respect is the evaluator's plan or action to be more diligent or more nearly perfect than is "reasonable. . . in the circumstances." One functional consequence of the Standards, then, is to foster community among evaluators by promulgating a spirit of tolerance—a spirit that is not the usual companion of high-mindedness.

Ostensibly, the ERS document is the opposite of restrictive, welcoming the greatest variety of evaluation approaches. Five broad categories of inquiry are recognized as aspects of program evaluation. By implication, the document denies that measuring effect size is primary and that all other inquiry is of lesser value, and it puts behind us the notion that there is one best design for an evaluation. A door is left ajar for impact evaluations that do not focus on goal attainment (although the document does not speak wholeheartedly on that point).

The Standards are unlikely to restrain trade directly. It would be impossible, I think, for a regulator to convert them into a scorecard for an evaluation or a set of evaluations. Almost all the document constitutes a call for fuller communication. It says that evaluators should plan deliberately and should be prepared to give their reasons for each choice. The document does not place a greater burden of proof on particular choices (for example, of a case study over a quantitative survey). This amounts to an outright rejection—no less important for being silent—of efforts to improve evaluation by imposing academic standards.

It is unfortunate that the attempt to be both high-minded and permissive leaves some sentences so general as to suggest that some issues were not faced squarely. I am inclined to think that attempts to be more definite would have come to naught, because there are defensible options at almost every step in an evaluation, and, with regard to a particular option, the balance of costs and benefits changes from one evaluation to the next. Indeed, it may never become possible to make explicit the contingencies under which, for example, information should be collected from or on uncooperative subjects (in violation of standard 18).

In sum, the Standards lack bite, and their contribution lies mostly in the symbolism of their existence. Beyond that, they tell evaluators to concern themselves with financial accountability, subjects' rights, documentation of the steps from data to conclusions, clarity of communication, and so on, not solely with research operations. These reminders can raise consciousness in evaluators who conceive of their roles too narrowly. Also, they can strengthen the hand of evaluators in negotiating with sponsors who are insensitive to one or another of these ideals.

Unvoiced Messages

The Standards subtly encourage some evaluation approaches over others. This imbalance probably arises from the inevitable character of standards. Standards purport to convey directives for action, not mere sentiments, and it is far easier to make explicit recommendations on some topics than on others. An unintended weighting results, which throws the resulting standards out of balance. What, then, is the slant of these Standards?

The ERS document is aligned more with Wholey's (1979) views than with those of any other recent position statement on evalution. Wholey sees evaluation primarily as a service to officials and the impetus of evaluation as arising from what officials want to know. In these Standards, the agency contracting for the evaluation is referred to as "the client" (standard 17). Is not the true client a pluralistic policy-shaping community and the sponsor merely its agent in buying information (Cronbach and Associates, 1980)? The ERS Standards state that "the parties to the evaluation" are asked to come to a mutual understanding; this phrase seems not to include persons who are served by the program or persons who will be affected by decisions. House, Scriven, and some of the rest of us have stressed the evaluator's special responsibility to introduce questions that officials overlook or prefer not to have investigated. The Standards admit "the public interest" (standard 2) only in a grudging way that surely has in mind only the abstract, generalized public, not fragmented constituencies and categories of clients.

Significant content is conveyed by what the Standards do not say. The first such message is that evaluators have no reason to concern themselves with values; the word *values* does not appear in the document. Yet, evaluators could reasonably take as a primary task the identification of value issues pertinent to a program.

Although the Standards are called standards for evaluation, these are in truth standards of conduct for evaluators. What about the conduct of sponsors? A few references to clarity in negotiating the contract (standards 5 and 7) seem to place symmetric responsiblity on sponsor and evaluator. Beyond that, however, the Standards Committee did not choose to put a finger on acts of sponsors that impair evaluations. Even a few timorous platitudes about good sponsor behavior would serve as an entering wedge for things that the profession should be starting to say. The following standard — a suggestion that I do not expect to have accepted as worded here — exemplifies what I think is missing:

Unless restriction of reports has been agreed on in advance, the sponsor should release the evaluator's report, as written, within two months of its delivery. The sponsor may appropriately provide comments on an earlier draft for the evaluator's consideration and may appropriately release its own interpretation alongside the report.

The kernel of the ERS document is the Standards proper. The prefatory remarks—a kind of outer wrapping—will receive less attention than the kernel; their less hortatory tone gives their content the weight of a footnote. This would not matter if forematter and text were in accord, but they are not. That is, the forematter expresses an awareness that is imperceptible in the Standards proper.

Whereas the Standards speak throughout of "the evaluation," reference to an evaluation "program" (found only in a preamble) is more in keeping with recent writings. Studies on utilization indicate that it is rare for an outcome evaluation to stimulate large change in the particular service studied. Evaluations are used, in the sense that officials draw thoughts about general policy from the whole emerging corpus of social research, including evaluations. It, therefore, is wise to plan not separate evaluations but a portfolio of studies with overlapping time schedules. Such planning calls for the collective wisdom of sponsoring agencies, social scientists, and concerned citizens (Cronbach and Associates, 1980). None of us is yet clear about the implications of this recent insight for investment in evaluation, but for the Standards to reduce the notion of investigative programs to a single word—printed, as it were, on the wrapper—is a shortcoming.

The preamble gives adequate emphasis to the study of process, of the interconnected events in the setting, delivery, reception, and sequelae of the social service. We do, indeed, need to ask how things work, whether or not we can agree on how well they work. Unfortunately, the word *process* is absent from the Standards proper (and the word *explanation* appears nowhere).

Concern for cause-and-effect relationships does appear (standards 6 and 38). The evaluator who chooses to make a causal statement is directed to "eliminate" plausible rival hypotheses (standard 38). This—one of the few standards that actually issues a command—asks too much. A given design will make some counterexplanations less plausible, but even a strongly controlled design cannot provide certainty regarding the meaning of any one study (Cook and Campbell, 1979, p. 83). Here, in the endorsement of evaluability assessment as a preliminary (standard 6) and in the call for a no-treatment control group or a surrogate in the outcome-oriented study (standard 14), the Standards strongly suggest that evaluators should be concerned with "treatment made a difference" conclusions. Hence, the Standards themselves are less liberal than the preamble.

Standard 6 misconstrues one of Wholey's (1979) main themes. For him, evaluability assessment is not a preliminary; it comes at the end of substantial evaluation activity. One by-product of that inquiry is a recommendation for or against undertaking a formal summative study. For Wholey, the comparative study will most often be a comparison of pretested treatment alternatives. The kernel seems to be preoccupied with old-fashioned treatment–no-treatment null hypotheses at a time when many are calling for studies that trace processes and contingencies to their conclusions. To restore balance, the ERS Standards should include standards intended to invite and strengthen process studies. For openers, I suggest these two:

1. The evaluator should try to make sense of any numerical result.
2. The evaluator should try to explain why outcomes within a treatment differ from site to site.

Process standards probably have to be nebulous. That they are absent from the ERS Standards reflects the natural tendency of standard setters to speak only of the more formal, standardizable aspects of their subject.

Once an evaluation begins, information is brought back from the field—some of it unanticipated. Then, there should be reconsideration and revision of the priorities assigned to evaluation questions and the plans for inquiry. The preamble says this, but the theme receives only a backhanded, passive reference in the Standards themselves (standard 11). The Standards proper are committed to prespecification of evalution purposes, questions, and procedures. The first two sections, which have to do with the launching of the evaluation, contain eighteen standards. Ten of these ask that something be "specified" or "made clear" or "described and justified"; not one suggests that something could be left open for later consideration. Of course, evaluators should plan and specify and make clear; what I miss is a modifier—for example, "tentative" or "preliminary and incomplete."

"The approach to a case study," we are told, "is as subject to specification as the design of an experimental study." The remark is true in a whimsical sense, because an intelligent field experiment is subject to little prespecification. In a number of true experiments that started with impartial allocation of subjects to treatment groups, the inquiries paid off primarily because the investigators thought freshly about the data as they came in. Often, the experimental manipulation played the role only of increasing the range of a variable, such as food intake or income; the analyst regrouped cases on the actual extent of service or food or income received, without regard to ostensible assignment, in order to bring out more basic phenomena. (See Cronbach, 1982, on this and many other matters on which I question the Standards.)

Construct Validation: Where Art Thou?

The Standards' remarks on validity are off target. The validity of each measurement method should be "estimated" (standards 16 and 23); and should the evaluator not consider the validity of interpretations, rather than of measurements? And, does an estimate not call for a number? Although a regression coefficient can play some part in justifying an employment practice, validating an interpretation of any kind is a qualitative, judgmental process. The interpreter can do no more than lay out an argument defending the interpretation; its plausibility is for the audience to determine (Cronbach and Associates, 1980; House, 1980; Messick, 1981).

Validity in evaluation is almost always of the construct sort. The issue is whether indicators collected by another procedure (and on another realization of the treatment concept) would—when put "in language understandable by" the audience (standard 41)—lead to the same conclusion. The writers of the Standards seem never to have heard of construct validity as the term is applied to evaluation by Cook and Campbell (1979). My sympathetic guess is that their hearts were in the right place, but they found it impossible to write crisp one-sentence regulations for subtle reasoning activities.

Evaluators should be self-critical. They should ask whether the data are biased by respondents' desire to speak well of a service lest it be discontinued or by the overloading of an educational outcome measure with tasks on which one of the competing instructional programs concentrated. Treatment events as well as instruments require this scrutiny. It is an error to regard schools funded by a certain program as treated and schools that received no such funds as untreated. Many school superintendents draw funds from a second source to get innovation into control schools. Demonstrating that this did not happen is a validity study as much as any check on an instrument is.

Construct validation consists of an attempt to falsify a proposed interpretation. The evaluator identifies plausible rival hypotheses and looks for evidence that would support them, hoping not to find it. Because time is limited and rival interpretations are inexhaustible, validation cannot be thorough. An adequate standard would stop with a request for the evaluator, before and after collecting data, to think about possible contaminants. Of course, a multimethod procedure (multiple realizations of treatments as well as multiple indicators) in commendable, but I am pleased that the Standards do not call for it.

The art of design is to decide when and how to make each such investment, as the investment inevitably diverts resources from another aspect of the inquiry. The call for information on reliability in these same Standards (standards 16 and 23) is stereotyped, and it could be misread. The right question is whether the sample statistics, not individual measurements, are reliable—standard errors are what matter. Procedures that have unimpressive reliability coefficients can be entirely satisfactory for a conclusion based on group means. The Standards rightly do not say that all instruments should have high reliability; their silence contains wisdom that most readers will overlook.

Concluding Comments

The preamble emphasizes that the Standards will change and grow. This change may take the form of increasingly detailed advice. It is said that, as the Standards are used, "examples of acceptable practices" will accumulate as material for a later edition. The hint that some practices are unacceptable makes me uneasy. To be sure, fiscal irresponsibility, for example, is unacceptable. But, in the areas to which most of my comments have been directed, another mode of extension may work to our advantage. Could we not have examples in which different evaluators have followed (or advocated) different courses of action with regard to, for example, extent of quality control? Describing these divergent positions and the arguments for each would make explicit the extent to which evaluation decisions are contingent. That would enhance the educational power of the document and avoid holding up a practice that was right in one circumstance as a model for most circumstances.

These Standards will do little to standardize evaluations, and it will be extremely difficult to use them as a checklist in approving or disapproving an evaluation plan. We should all be grateful for the wisdom and effort that brought about such a happy result.

References

American Psychological Association. *Technical Recommendations for Psychological Tests and Diagnostic Techniques.* Washington, D.C.: American Psychological Association, 1954.
American Psychological Association. *Standards for Educational and Psychological Tests.* Washington, D.C.: American Psychological Association, 1974.
Cook, T., and Campbell, D. T. *Quasi-Experimentation.* Chicago: Rand-McNally, 1979.
Cronbach, L. J. *Designing Evaluations of Educational and Social Programs.* San Francisco: Jossey-Bass, 1982.
Cronbach, L. J., and Associates. *Toward Reform of Program Evaluation: Aims, Methods, and Institutional Arrangements.* San Francisco: Jossey-Bass, 1980.

58

Descartes, R. *The Philosophical Works of Descartes Rendered into English.* Vol. 1. Cambridge, England: Cambridge University Press, 1969. (Originally published 1637.)

House, E. *Evaluating with Validity.* Beverly Hills, Calif.: Sage, 1980.

Messick, S. "Evidence and Ethics in the Evaluation of Tests." *Educational Researcher,* 1981, *10* (10), 9-20.

Wholey, J. S. *Evaluation: Promise and Performance.* Washington, D.C.: Urban Institute, 1979.

Lee J. Cronbach is a former professor of education, having retired from Stanford University in 1980. The author of Designing Evaluations of Educational and Social Programs *(Jossey-Bass, 1982), he was chairman of the committee that developed the original version of the American Psychological Association test standards in 1951–1954.*

*The dilemma inherent in all formal standards results from
the tension between maintaining quality control, on the one hand,
and constraining creativity, on the other.*

Where Angels Fear
to Tread and Why

Richard A. Berk

If the recent Standards for Program Evaluation are taken seriously, many aspects of program evaluation may well be affected. In particular, there will be
increased pressure toward homogeneity; decision makers will share increasingly similar understandings about the nature of evaluation research, RFPs
will reflect a set of common concerns, evaluators will at least pretend to proceed by the (now) conventional methods, students in evaluation will be ex-
posed to "accepted procedure," and the like. For individuals who feel that
much of evaluation research has foundered on indolence, incompetence, or
chicanery, standards are a good thing. Standards presume to place a floor beneath which evaluation quality will not fall. Unfortunately, standards can also
constrain the activities of evaluators at the upper end of the distribution, especially when boilerplate practice will not suffice. Acceptable procedures may so
circumscribe evaluation practice that innovation and creativity will suffer. Put
a bit grandly, the many guidelines appear to force a choice between the spirit
of Galileo and the specter of Cyril Burt.

Perhaps nowhere does the trade-off become more apparent than in
matters of method: measurement, sampling, research design, and statistical
analysis. As I propose to demonstrate here, even for that aspect of evaluation

P. Rossi (Ed.). *New Directions for Program Evaluation: Standards for Evaluation Practice,* no. 15.
San Francisco: Jossey-Bass, September 1982.

60

research where the concept of standards seems to make the most sense, the tension between homogeneity and innovation is very real. I will suggest, however, that there are ways in which the Standards for Program Evaluation can be revised so as to make the game somewhat less zero-sum.

How Do the Standards Constrain Methodological Innovation?

Any set of standards assumes that, as a practical matter, it is possible to distinguish between proper and improper behavior. At least at the extremes, good and bad are empirically distinct. A priori, one might suppose that this holds most clearly for technical matters. Surely, it must be an easy task to determine, for example, whether "analytic procedures [are] appropriate to the properties of the measures used and to the quality and quantity of the data" (standard 33). In fact, it often is not.

What If Nobody Knows? For many of the technical procedures used in evaluation research, substantial ignorance prevails. For example, many of our most popular statistical techniques are formally justified by the properties of maximum likelihood estimators. Thus, the significance tests associated with analytic methods that are most appropriate for analyses of nominal outcomes (for example, arrested or not, dropped out of school or not, became ill or not) typically have unknown validity in small samples; except under very special circumstances, logit and probit techniques rely on sampling distributions whose properties are known only asymptotically (see, for example, Judge and others, 1980, Chapter 14). In empirical work, of course, our samples are finite, which raises two related questions: First, how large does a sample have to be before asymptotic properties are safely approximated? Second, what credence should be given to statistical inference when the sample is less than large (for example, less than 100)? There are no general answers available, and even answers specific to the data on hand depend on knowing things about the data that it is typically impossible to determine.

The small sample properties of maximum likelihood estimators are but one example of the ignorance that prevails even in technical matters. There is no best way, for instance, to respond to multicollinearity, outliers, missing data, or the detection of specification errors. How, then, do we normally proceed? Unless the evaluator happens to be interested in the technical side of things per se, proper procedures will often rest on convention. Later evaluations will be undertaken much like early evaluations.

Reliance on precedent in a state of ignorance is not necessarily bad. There is at least some chance that studies will be comparable. However, one faces the genuine risk that conventional practice will be misunderstood as correct practice, and the problem is compounded if such confusion is realized in the application of standards or even in the standards themselves.

More worrisome, strong institutional pressures may be supporting conventions that have no particular scientific merit. In a world that is skeptical about program evaluation, some may feel that our ignorance should be a private matter. Any evaluator, therefore, who has the temerity openly to try something unconventional risks a serious reprimand — or worse.

What If Nobody Knows, but Some Claim They Do? Some readers may feel that the scenario just described is very unlikely. These readers should consider that the same consequences follow from other circumstances as well. Consider the following example. In his justly famous and classic article, "Reforms as Experiments," Donald T. Campbell (1969) asserts that the applicability of regression-discontinuity designs is necessarily constrained because of problems introduced by ties. In recent work, however, Goldberger (1972), Barnow (1975), and others have proved that the problems identified by Campbell are not really problems at all.

Imagine the outcome if, in 1970, some evaluator had employed a regression-discontinuity design counter to Campbell's warnings. Suppose also that, after presenting findings based on an analysis of covariance, our evaluator is challenged under either standard 33 or under standard 31: "The analytic procedures should be matched to the purposes of the evaluation, the design, and the data collection." In particular, the evaluator claims that the analysis of covariance, coupled with the research design, guarantees that unbiased estimates of the treatment effect are obtained for the full range of the covariate. The program manager, citing Campbell, disagrees and asks for censure under the Standards for Program Evaluation. What chance would the evaluator have against the published views of Donald T. Campbell (who would, of course, be appalled if his work were used in this manner)? Perhaps the evaluator would eventually prevail, especially if he or she could produce the requisite proofs, which were not in the public domain in 1970. However, vindication would surely incur significant costs, and the deterrent value of the experience is clear. Simply put, even in the absence of a Standards inquisition, there would be clear incentives not to rock the boat; Campbell has defined the right and the wrong, and violators, therefore, proceed at their own risk.

What If It Is Only Possible to Know in Theory? In the face of methodological problems, it is often easy to find textbook solutions that are at least adequate, if not optimal, and that are widely recognized as such. Under these circumstances, the complications just described may not arise. However, the Standards for Program Evaluation must still respond to the kinds of trade-offs inherent in real-world applications.

On the one hand, there are frustrating trade-offs between purely technical decisions. Given a fixed amount of research funding, how much internal validity, for instance, should be traded for how much external validity? In particular, would it be appropriate to use an interrupted time-series design instead of a randomized experiment if data could be obtained on a representative sample of program participants instead of just on the group that volunteered for random assignment? Likewise, to what extent is one prepared to introduce statistical bias into one's results for greater statistical efficiency? More concretely, would a better evaluation follow from a randomized experiment with a sample of 100 or from causal modeling with a sample of 1,000? The general point is that such choices are inevitable in a world of finite resources and, yet, the precise trade-offs are not easy to determine. Even when the general nature of the compromise is known, there rarely exists a common metric with which to make informed judgments. What common metric do internal and external validity share?

On the other hand, there are trade-offs that are at least as troubling between technical matters and other concerns. Examples are easy to construct: The most internally valid research design may be risky on political grounds; the most efficient statistical procedures may be very expensive to compute; and the most accurate measures may threaten the privacy of subjects.

In many settings, therefore, one might choose to weaken the technical side of an evaluation in order to serve other priorities. But how, then, can the technical quality of an evaluation be properly determined? Occasionally, the trade-offs are clear, and all reasonable parties will agree on the best procedures. For example, statutes may prohibit the collection of the most desirable data, and it is unlikely that evaluators will be chastised for collecting flawed data when the alternative risks a fine or imprisonment.

Yet, it is more common that the trade-offs are not clear. As a result, application of evaluation research technology will often rest heavily on judgment calls between incommensurate alternatives. Even if the benefits and costs that follow from contrasting research strategies can be known in advance (and one could settle for the probability distribution of these benefits and costs), it is not at all apparent how a summary judgment could be made. What common units are shared by random measurement error (even translated into biased estimates, if that could be determined) and breaches of confidentiality? Perhaps both could be monetized, but it is hard to imagine that a widely accepted exchange value between the two would be forthcoming.

To the degree that many of the technical guidelines in the Standards for Program Evaluation cannot withstand the problems posed by practical applications, it might appear that here, at least, the Galileos of the evaluation enterprise would be allowed to flourish. Without raising the larger question of what purpose the Standards might then have, I will observe that the Standards are an open invitation to moral entrepreneurs who will turn particular guidelines towards inappropriate ends. I am reminded especially of recent experiences on campuses across the country with committees designed to protect the rights of human subjects. Far too often, these committees have become the private preserve of academics who lack the technical expertise properly to consider the research before them. Often, these individuals came from disciplines, such as law, that prejudged many of the inherent trade-offs, or they held substantive biases against certain kinds of research, or they used the committee to reward friends and punish enemies, or they simply got caught up in the puffery that one can build into a job of this nature. I fear that many of the technical guidelines in the Standards provide similar opportunities. The Galileos are still in some jeopardy.

How Might the Standards Be Improved?

No set of evaluation research standards can satisfy everyone, and no set of evaluation research standards can be flawless.

One of my criticisms of the ERS Standards is that their methodological guidelines appear to lack underlying principles to explain why some standards are very broad and some very narrow. Moreover, looking only at the narrow standards, I am unable to determine why these were chosen, when others that seem equally important were neglected. Reliable measures, for example, are surely a good thing, but so are probability samples, analyses of outliers, and accurate computational algorithms. Nevertheless, at least when methodological matters are considered, it seems rather easy to improve the Standards for Program Evaluation.

First, the tone of the technical guidelines needs to be modified. There should be full acknowledgement that often there are no right answers and that trade-offs and judgment calls are inherent in the enterprise. There should also be statements encouraging innovation; surely, a discipline committed to social experimentation should support experimentation within its own ranks.

Second, in the context of support for methodological flexibility and innovation, the guidelines should be described as establishing certain burdens of proof. Inventiveness without discipline, replicability, and reference to past practice comes perilously close to unfettered license. The Standards, therefore, can be seen as demanding that nontrivial deviations from conventional approaches require extra justification; the burden of proof falls on the innovator.

At the same time, this burden should not be punitive, arbitrary, or capricious. Thus, the standards of proof for innovations should be no higher than the standards of proof for business as usual. For example, if the only justifications for some set of conventional statistical procedures rest on Monte Carlo simulations, formal proofs should not be required for the new perspective. Recall the regression-discontinuity example. In 1970, many of Campbell's assertions about regression-discontinuity designs were stated in an intuitive manner, without formal proof. A challenger, consequently, should have been able to propose alternatives resting on comparable rigor.

It should also not be necessary to demonstrate that a new approach is superior to past practice. Equal merit should suffice. Referring again to an earlier example, if there is little to choose between logit and probit approaches for nominal endogenous variables, both should be equally acceptable; conventional preferences should be irrelevant. My argument here is that one should encourage innovation, even if that risks reducing comparability across evaluation studies.

Third, some of the methodological guidelines are far too broad to be instructive. While this might be justified on just the sort of grounds advanced in this chapter, there are many instances in which increased specificity is both possible and desirable. In particular, it is a simple matter to formulate technical guidelines that seem to pose no threat to flexibility and innovation and that still seem to capture important aspects of sound methodological practice. Examples include the following:

1. Response rates should be calculated and reported for all evaluations resting on survey data.

2. The potential role of sample selection bias should be analyzed and reported.

3. Analyses of attrition should be routinely undertaken and reported.

4. The impact of outliers should be routinely analyzed and reported.

5. The assumptions underlying all statistical procedures should be reviewed and reported.

6. The likelihood that these assumptions are violated should be reported, along with the possible consequences of these violations.

7. Results based on a priori theory and model specifications should be clearly distinguished from results resting of post hoc models and exploratory analyses.

8. Results resting on multiple significance tests should be properly discounted, or at least the fact that multiple tests have been undertaken should be reported.

9. Procedures used for missing data should be reported and critically reviewed.

10. Computer programs used at any stage of the research should be described, along with any suspected problems (for example, vulnerability to rounding errors).

These technical guidelines are hardly exhaustive. Those given here are meant primarily to illustrate three underlying principles. First, a critical feature of sound evaluation practice is concern for all the things that can go wrong. Thus, the Standards should serve in part as an early-warning system for hazards that need to be anticipated. It is also important to emphasize that the early-warning system functions for the well-being of the evaluator and the policymaker. In essence, methodological standards like the ten just listed provide a checklist of difficulties that a sound evaluation must address.

Second, to the extent that the Standards flag potential difficulties, the evaluator is responsible for explaining whether the problems are real for the study in question, how this determination has been made, what actions (if any) have been taken, and what consequences might follow for the credibility of the results. Note that these sorts of technical issues need not be (and probably should not be) fully discussed in executive summaries or overview chapters. However, important implications for evaluation findings should be included in those sections of reports likely to be of primary interest to policy makers and backed up with technical sections for individuals who want to pursue such matters in depth.

Third, the ten illustrative guidelines proposed raise potential problems, but they do not prescribe particular solutions. Innovation, therefore, should not be inhibited, indeed, by alerting evaluators to possible complications for which ready remedies are often lacking, methodological creativity is actually being encouraged. However, evaluators who fail to consider one or more of the methodological pitfalls listed in the Standards are in principle required to provide special justifications (consistent with where the burden of proof lies) if their activities are challenged.

Finally, the methodological standards proposed here as examples go well beyond broad admonitions to do good. They represent the kinds of problems that one commonly finds indexed in respectable statistics texts and that readily lead to rich technical literatures, to which readers may refer for specific guidance.

References

Barnow, B. S. "The Effect of Head Start and Socioeconomic Status on Cognitive Development of Disadvantaged Children." Unpublished doctoral dissertation, University of Wisconsin, 1975.

Campbell, D. T. "Reforms as Experiments," *American Psychologist,* April 1969, 409-429.

Goldberger, A. S. "Selection Bias in Evaluating Treatment Effects: Some Formal Illustrations" (Discussion Paper 123–172). Madison: University of Wisconsin, Institute for Research on Poverty, 1972.

Judge, G. G., and others. *Theory and Practice of Econometrics.* New York: Wiley, 1980.

Richard A. Berk is professor of sociology at the University of California, Santa Barbara. He is the coauthor (with Peter Rossi and Kenneth Lenihan) of Money, Work, and Crime: Experimental Evidence *(Academic Press).*

If the ERS Standards for Program Evaluation are to improve
evaluation practices, proposal review, prerelease critiques,
summative assessments, and secondary analysis may be necessary.

An Assessment of the Utility
of the ERS Standards

David S. Cordray

On June 30, 1980, Boruch and Cordray (1980) submitted a report to the
Congress and Department of Education containing recommendations for improving evaluation practices at local, state, and federal levels of governance.
In that report, we point out the potential of recently developed standards as
means of enhancing the quality of evaluation evidence. The standards and
guidelines considered include those issued by the Joint Committee on Standards for Educational Evaluation (1980), the U.S. General Accounting Office
(1978), the Evaluation Research Society (1980), and others.

This chapter focuses on why and how standards might be incorporated
into the evaluation process. Two themes are explored: the extent to which the
ERS Standards differ from other recent standards-setting activities and their
applicability to local and state-level evaluation efforts. The final section enumerates some impending issues regarding their use and ongoing development.

Support for this chapter was provided by grant #G-79-0128 from the National
Institute of Education. I would like to thank Lee Sechrest, Georgine Pion, and Robert
F. Boruch for comments on an earlier draft.

P. Rossi (Ed.). *New Directions for Program Evaluation: Standards for Evaluation Practice,* no. 15.
San Francisco: Jossey-Bass, September 1982.

Rationale for Standards

Rationale for Standards. In describing why standards are necessary, we (Boruch and Cordray, 1980; Boruch and others, 1981) noted the extensive ambiguity in the way such terms as "evaluation," "effectiveness," and "impact" are used in law, regulation, evaluation reports, and face-to-face conversations. The standards that we reviewed seem to provide a solid basis for disentangling lexical ambiguity about evaluation by specifying concrete practices focused on audience, object, and issue identification. We argued that evaluation standards should not be incorporated into law. Rather, we recommended that Congress use the standards to understand what can reasonably be expected of evaluations; direct agencies to use them where appropriate, as a guide for developing criteria to judge evaluation plans submitted by local education agencies (LEAs) and state education agencies (SEAs); and elicit assistance in interpreting standards from the groups that have been instrumental in their construction.

The fact that the quality of evaluation efforts varies enormously (Cook and Gruder, 1978) also argues for the establishment of standards and guidelines. For example, Lyon and others (1978) concluded that even simple standards were not uniformly adhered to in reports issued by large school districts. Their evidence suggests that evaluation reports often do not describe program implementation, address issues of reliability and validity of data sources, or connect the evidence with the conclusions. What appeared to be best about the reports studied is that the majority identified program and evaluation participants, data collection sources, data analysis procedures, and results. Whether these evaluations failed to report the missing evidence or failed to collect it is not known. Our review of LEA evaluations suggests that reporting standards can provide guides to the quality of evidence that is offered (Cordray, Boruch, and Pion, 1980). But, as already indicated, we suggest that assistance in interpreting standards is sometimes necessary. Judging from published commentary on standards, our concern over the potential for ambiguity seems warranted.

Ambiguity in Their Purpose. A few moments of consultation with the *Oxford English Dictionary* reveals numerous uses for the word *standard.* Nearly three and one-half pages are devoted to the origins and definitions of the word. In these pages, we find that a standard can be synonymous with a flag, emblem, example, criteria, rule, or model. However, the potential for ambiguity is better represented by the presence of commentary in the evaluation literature regarding other standards-setting efforts (for example, Joint Committee on Standards for Educational Evaluation, 1980). The diversity of opinion about the utility of standards suggests that professional researchers hold different notions about the meaning of the term. For example, Stake (1981) outlines four questions concerning efforts to establish standards. His questions deal with the degree of specificity and uniformity of standards, what to do with offenders, and whether a profession should try to control its members. The tone of Stake's discussion and the focus of his questions imply that he views standard setting as rule making.

In contrast, Sechrest (1981), also commenting on the Joint Committee Standards, states that "all standards are essentially moral prescriptions, and, like any set of commandments, they are easier to state than to follow" (p. 146). Sechrest's tone implies that standards are more akin to a model of what is judged to be good conduct and something towards which we should aspire. However, Sechrest also makes reference to the requirements established by the Joint Committee Standards, and he expresses some concern that they did not include some of the elements implicit (or explicit) within his model of proper evaluation conduct.

Becker and Kirkhart (1981) draw out the implications of the Standards for professional licensure and accreditation. They state that "the Standards could be used as a starting point for developing criteria for licensing [and] accreditation" (p. 154). The Standards could be used for guiding the development of training programs, for constructing standardized tests for licensing and accreditation, and for judging an evaluator's performance. These authors appear to view the efforts of the Joint Committee on Standards as a set of minimum criteria. A similar argument can be offered as a rationale for the ESEA Title I Evaluation and Reporting System (TIERS) (Anderson and others, 1978). In this instance, compliance defines what is acceptable, but evaluation personnel at state and local levels are encouraged to engage in activities beyond those specified by the TIERS requirements.

While each of these interpretations of the role of standard setting (that is, minimum criteria, model, or rules) serves as a context for understanding professional reactions to such efforts, it seems prudent to examine them relative to the intent of their initiators.

ERS Standards: Content and Scope

Some standards and guildelines are, by necessity, explicit as to what is required for minimum compliance (for example, the ESEA Title I Evaluation and Reporting System). The Evaluation Research Society Standards (Evaluation Research Society, 1981) were originally conceived as being general guidelines for improving evaluation practice. As such, they represent generic evaluation concerns applicable to the broad disciplinary representation of the ERS membership. The authors claim that these standards have been influenced by the other standards-setting efforts, but they are applicable to a broader range of evaluation activities and disciplines. Given the published commentary on the Joint Committee Standards, particularly those focused on overspecification (Stake, 1981) and omissions (Sechrest, 1981), and our claims that the different standards show a remarkable degree of consistency (Boruch and Cordray, 1980; Cordray 1981), a more systematic appraisal of the overlap among them seems warranted.

The first level of appraisal amounts to an admittedly simplistic comparison of the content of three sets of standards: those issued by the ERS, those of the Joint Committee on Educational Evaluation, and those of the General Accounting Office (GAO). This comparison appears in Table 1. Since a content analysis of this sort tends to ignore differences in emphasis and detail, a second level of appraisal, which is more specific and uses criteria for judging the value of standards as a guide for professional conduct (Chalk, Frankel and Chafer, 1980) is also offered.

A Comparative Assessment. Table 1 enumerates the issues addressed in the ERS Standards and designates the corresponding standards from the Joint Committee on Standards for Educational Evaluation (1980) and those issued by the General Accounting Office (1978). The Joint Committee's format is considerably different from that of the ERS and the GAO standards. Rather than offering guidance on practice in terms of the order with which issues typically arise in the evaluation context, the Joint Committee's standards are organized under four major topics: Utility, Feasibility, Propriety, and Accuracy. In total, thirty standards are offered. To facilitate interpretation of these standards, 178 guidelines are also delineated, along with pitfalls and caveats. If we count all the issues raised by the Joint Committee (that is, standards, guidelines, pitfalls, and caveats), a total of 369 pieces of advice are offered as to the proper conduct of educational evaluation.

The GAO standards, issued as an exposure draft in 1978, are specifically designed to guide and assess impact evaluations. As such, the GAO standards are more modest in the number and types of issues raised. Even with this limited focus, fifty items are enumerated. Similar to the ERS Standards, these are presumably applicable for evaluations pertinent to a broad range of social interventions. Their organization is similar to that of the ERS document. They include standards for planning, data collection, data analysis, reporting results, and data disclosure. The topical organization of the ERS Standards appears as part of Table 1.

Looking at the content of the three sets of standards, there appears to be a consensus (across standard setters) as to how evaluations should be devised, executed, and disclosed. Further, as a means of making clear what sensible steps of an evaluation ought to be, the standards issued by ERS, the Joint Committee, and the GAO are in accord. Their content is diverse and should

Table 1. Comparison of the Content of the Standards Issued by the Evaluation Research Society (ERS), Joint Committee on Standards for Educational Evaluation, and General Accounting Office (GAO)

	ERS	*Joint Committee*	*GAO*
FORMULATION AND NEGOTIATION			
1. Purposes and characteristics of the program		D1	A2.1-A2.3
2. Audience, needs and expectations		A1	A1.1-A1.3
3. Type, objectives, range of activities for evaluation		A3 A4	A1.4 A3 A7.1 A7.2
4. Sound, prudent and ethically responsible cost estimate		C8	*
5. Cost-benefit of evaluative information		B3	*
6. Feasibility of the evaluation		B1 B2	A2.1-A2.4 A7.1-A7.4 A8
7. Restrictions on data access or dissemination		C4	E2.2
8. Conflict of interest		C2	*
9. Rights and welfare of parties		C5	E2.2
10. Technical and financial accountability		C8	*
11. Formal agreements		C1	A7.4 A8.1 A8.2
12. Capabilities		A2	B1.2 B1.3 B1.5
STRUCTURE AND DESIGN			
13. Approach to evaluation		A4	A3.2 A3.4 D1.4
14. Estimating effects		D8	A3.4 C1.1-C1.3 C3 A4.1
15. Sampling methods		D4	A4.2 A4.3 A6 C2
16. Reliability and validity of measures		D5 D6	A5 A6
17. Appropriateness of procedures and instruments		D3 D5 D6	A3.1 A3.2 A6
18. Cooperation		C1	A8.1 A8.2
DATA COLLECTION AND PREPARATION			
19. Data collection and preparation plan		*	*
20. Departures from original plan		D7	E1.1
21. Staff competency		D7 A2	B1.2 B1.3 B1.5
22. Preservation of human dignity		C6	*
23. Verification of reliability and validity		D4 D5 D6	A5
24. Sources of errors		D7	B1.6 B1.7 B2.1
25. Biased data collection		D7 D11	A5
26. Minimum disruption		B1	*
27. Risks and informed consent		C5	*
28. Unauthorized release		C5	E2.2 E2.1
29. Complete documentation		D4	E1.2
30. Irrecoverable loss of data		*	*

Table 1. Comparison of the Content of the Standards Issued by the Evaluation Research Society (ERS), Joint Committee on Standards for Educational Evaluation, and General Accounting Office (GAO) *(continued)*

ERS	Joint Committee	GAO
DATA ANALYSIS AND INTERPRETATION		
31. Analysis	D8 D9	C1.1-C1.3
32. Assumptions and analytic procedures	A4 D8 D9	A3.3 C3 D1.3
33. Appropriateness of analysis	D8 D9	C1.1-C1.3
34. Unit of analysis	D8 D9	C2
35. Analysis -- justification	D8 D9	C1.1-C1.3
36. Documentation for replication	D8 D9	E1.2 E1.1
37. Statistical and practical significance	D8	*
38. Rival explanations	D8 D10	A3.4
39. Findings vs judgments/opinion	D11 C3	D1.1-D1.5
COMMUNICATION AND DISCLOSURE		
40. Findings -- clarity, fairness and completeness	A5 C3	D1.1-D1.5
41. Clarity of language	A5	D1.1-D1.5
42. Findings and recommendations		D1.2
43. Assumptions - general	C3 C7 A4	D1.3
44. Limitations and need for further study	A8	D1.5 A7
45. How findings were derived	A4 A5 D3 D10	D1.4
46. Appropriate feedback	A6	D1.1
47. Disclosure procedures	C5	E2.2
48. Authorization for release	C5	E2.1
49. Organization of documentation	*	E1.2
USE OF RESULTS		
50. Timely dissemination	A7	A7.1
51. Misinterpretation and misuse	B2 D11	*
52. Side effects	C7	*
53. Distinguish findings from recommendations	A5	*
54. Recommendations - costs/benefits of alternatives	A8	*
55. Evaluator and advocacy roles	A8	*

Note: The Joint Committee Standards are organized into four major areas: There are 8 Utility Standards (designated as A1-A8); three Feasibility Standards (B1-B3), eight Proprietary Standards (C1-C8); and eleven Accuracy Standards (D1-D11). *The GAO standards are organized into five sections, most contain subparts (e.g., D1.2). Those pertinent to Evaluation Planning are designated as A1 to A8, Data Collection (B1-B2), Data Analysis (C1-C3), Reporting Results (D1-D3), and Data Disclosure (E1 and E2). Those standards that are not explicitly mentioned by The Joint Committee or GAO are designated with an asterisk (*).

defuse arguments about the sufficiency and the superiority of individual strategies (for example, case studies versus randomized experiments). The ERS Standards and the Joint Committee Standards are particularly good in this respect. In planning and executing an evaluation, practitioners are urged to collect multiple lines of evidence and establish the adequacy of methods used as a means of describing the object under consideration. Both sets of standards also call for selecting valid and reliable measures (qualitative and quantitative) and for establishing for the particular evaluation context the extent to which measures live up to these expectations. All this is balanced against their cost, client interest, response burden, and proprietary rights of clients, program participants, and researchers.

At a very general level, the members of the evaluation industry appear to have a model articulating what constitutes sound practice that crosses disciplinary boundaries and types of evaluation. The GAO standards are the most dissimilar (that is, they exhibit fewer areas of overlap) due to their unique focus on a special type of evaluation (namely, impact evaluation), and they are more an assessment device than they are a guide to practice.

Criteria for Judging Standards. Chalk, Frankel, and Chafer (1980) have systematically examined codes of ethics issued by a variety of professional societies. As part of their assessment, they provide a sensible list of criteria for judging the value of standards offered as guides for professional behavior. They enumerate six issues, which we may adapt to the assessment of standards. These six issues involve the extent to which standards are applicable to specific problems, are clearly specified, are internally consistent, allow priorities to be established, are comprehensive, and are acceptable.

Obviously, some of these issues (for example, acceptability) are empirical questions that can only be answered after the evaluation industry has accumulated considerable experience in the use of standards. We can, however, address some of these issues by examining their content in more detail. Table 1 shows a substantial degree of topical overlap among the three sets of standards. They diverge with respect to what is and what is not explicitly prescribed. For example, with regard to the comprehensiveness of the Joint Committee Standards, the use of high-quality research designs and specification of "fallback designs" (in the event of a failure to implement the preferred methods) is not explicitly recognized (Sechrest, 1981). Rather, the Joint Committee makes a passing reference to impact assessment in its standard on quantitative analysis. The ERS Standards are more complete in this regard, since they include a guideline on use and justification of the methods for estimating effects. The GAO standards are also direct in this regard, indicating concern over the statistical model and method of analysis pertinent to the data. None of the standards are explicit as to the importance of statistical power, but Mosteller, Gilbert, and McPeek (1980) have suggested incorporating power considerations into judgments on the quality of reported clinical trials in medical research. Perhaps the issue of power will be included in the next update of the various sets of standards.

Given the number of standards prescribed by each group, it is not likely that priorities will be easy to enumerate. Obtaining consensus, even for a specific evaluation project, can be even more elusive. All the standards seem to have this drawback. Specifying the sequence and cluster of issues within each stage of the evaluation process (as is done by the ERS Standards) may facilitate priority setting for each phase. The mechanics of these negotiation and formulation aspects of evaluation will probably require careful attention, as they are central to the structure and form assumed by the evaluation. I will return to this issue in my discussion of impending concerns.

Use of the Standards to Improve Practice

The basis for remarks in this section stem from the field research conducted as part of the Holtzman Project (Boruch and Cordray, 1980). The staff of this project relied on two general sources of information: contemporary investigations by other researchers and agencies and direct investigation. Direct investigation included twenty-two site visits to SEAs and LEAs and a telephone survey of approximately 200 LEAs. A stratified random sample was developed for site visits and for the larger telephone survey. The literature review covered published and unpublished documents, including reports maintained by ERIC; reports solicited from federal, state, and local agencies; and, in the case of statutes, the LEXIS system.

In an earlier paper (Cordray, 1981), I suggested three ways that standards could be used to promote higher-quality evaluations at the state and local levels as part of the program-planning process, as a basis for assessing the quality of the proposed evaluation effort prior to program funding decisions, and for two types of critique and review processes, namely prerelease and summative assessments.

Program-Planning Phase. The most ideal case for evaluation is when an intervention is planned in collaboration with those who will attempt to assess its operation and effectiveness. Due to time constraints, uncertainty regarding funding, limited resources, and the like, communication between program developers and evaluation personnel may not be initiated until the program funding decision has been made or, in some instances, after the program is operational. The ERS Standards, and for that matter the standards produced by the Joint Committee and the GAO, provide a useful framework for program developers. Articulating the general issues in a coherent document can serve as a guide to developers by identifying the types of issues that must be addressed when evaluators are ultimately drawn into a project. As such, the ERS Standards are not only prescriptions for evaluators but also a guide for developers about what they can expect from the individuals who are responsible for the planning, execution, and dissemination of results.

For example, standard 6 specifies an informal or formal feasibility assessment, which entails identifying constraints on the evaluation, necessary cooperation, and clarity of the program. Being forewarned of these issues, the program developers may be in a better position to inform the evaluator as to these constraints. Further, a conscientious program developer may be led by such standards to recognize that the initial program plan is infeasible and alter, sharpen, or abandon the original idea as a result. The forewarning function of the ERS Standards can also facilitate the negotiation and formulation processes by providing a basis for specifying issues in a RFP, thereby clarifying the type of information that the evaluator is requested to provide.

Proposal Review Process. The utility of the ERS Standards for program development and program specification as a means of promoting evaluation is fairly obvious. The Standards outline the salient evaluation issues and provide a common framework that allows program developers and evaluators to communicate more effectively, provided, or course, that each understands the issues involved. The use of standards as part of the program review process is less obvious and requires more elaboration. The basis for devoting explicit attention to the proposal review process stems from our examination of regulations for grant applications, which revealed that little emphasis is placed on the technical quality of evaluation plans. For certain grants (Boruch, Cordray, and Pion, 1981), no more than 15 percent of the total review points for a program proposal were devoted to the quality of the evaluation plan. Furthermore, the call for evaluation was often vague and of little use in developing an evaluation plan, especially for individuals with little or no expertise in evaluation. The incentives for seeking assistance from qualified personnel seem small, given the minor role that evaluation is afforded in the review process.

Not all evaluation requirements are vague; some explicitly designate the type of evaluation required. But, they are not necessarily consistent with good research practices. For example, the regulations for bilingual basic grants to LEAs specify use of a research design that provides "a comparison procedure to estimate what performance would have been in the absence of the project." However, the same regulations identify "historical or statistical comparisons" as adequate ways of deriving such an estimate. Such comparisons can be subject to biases that result in erroneous conclusions (Campbell and Boruch, 1975). While specifications about what evaluations should include seems desirable, deliberate efforts should be made to ensure that regulations do not encourage the use of weak strategies. Further, in the regulations that we reviewed, few focused in any explicit way on audience identification, provisions for critique and reanalysis, and documentation of the data file. Each of these practices is emphasized in the ERS Standards; each could be profitably included in regulations.

Prerelease Critique. Through site visits and telephone surveys, we solicited hundreds of evaluation reports, whose quality ranged from exceptional to clearly inadequate. Numerous reports that were filed had technical inadequacies, many of which could have been corrected easily if they had been identified by a conscientious external reviewer or an individual with technical common sense. Such review may be referred to as *prerelease critique.*

The benefit of conducting such reviews can be substantial. In one case, an evaluator described his procedures inaccurately, creating considerable confusion. In other cases, more serious errors were involved. An evaluation of the effects of a bilingual education project reported a *t*-test containing more degrees of freedom than the number of individuals tested; apparently, the investigator used an independent groups analysis, when the data were almost certainly correlated. Consistent with the data reported by Lyon and others (1978), failures to specify the object of the evaluation, purposes of the evaluation, and validity of the conclusions were also observed repeatedly. The routine use of an independent prerelease review should reduce the incidence of such inept reports.

Further, simply advocating the need for such a critique points to a major concern about the utility of standards. The ERS Standards (and others) request the evaluator to "describe and justify" the choice of analyses, designs, and measures that have been used to derive the conclusions that are offered. An evaluator may conscientiously fulfill these requirements and yet still fail to communicate to others the basic points. In the worst case, the evaluator may simply provide an erroneous justification. In the examples just cited, justifications for the analysis were indeed offered, but we questioned their technical soundness. If standards are to improve practice, an external review or audit clearly will be necessary. Minimally, the ERS Standards will serve to justify requests for additional information that can clarify the evaluation procedures, the description of the object under consideration, and the basis for the conclusions. In a sense, the prerelease critique can serve a function similar to that of editorial review for professional journals.

In many instances, program clients will have the technical common sense to detect obvious errors or misleading language. It seems more likely, however, that external audit (see Cordray, Boruch, and Pion, 1980), for examples) will be necessary. The drawback here is that such audit increases the cost of evaluation, and it must be planned for as part of the overall cost estimate. The ERS Standards are less explicit on the importance of a review of this nature and how it can be negotiated. The costs and benefits of such review will have to be weighed on a case-by-case basis.

Summative Assessments. While the prerelease review can ameliorate some of the obvious transgressions, inaccuracies, and leaps of faith that we observe, it will not compensate for poorly executed evaluations, nor will it necessarily establish the validity of a study. For this, we would recommend a second appraisal—a summative assessment. Specifically, once the primary analyst has provided the most complete set of descriptions and justifications for the conclusions that are offered (that is, the "best case," which takes client feedback or evaluation audit findings into account), a final review of the evaluation may be undertaken. Cook and Gruder (1978) suggest this type of review under the rubric of *metaevaluation.* The evaluation literature contains a number of studies in which the quality of several investigations is assessed at the same time (for example, Bernstein and Freeman, 1975; Gamel and others, 1975; Glass, 1978; Wargo and others, 1972) or quality of specific studies are examined (for example, House and others, 1978; Campbell and Erlebacher, 1970; Magidson, 1977). The primary purpose of summative review is to judge the extent to which the conclusions are justified, based on the evidence that is offered.

Independent evaluators may disagree as to the quality of evidence reported in a particular evaluation—a situation that is not uncommon, judging from published debates (Bowers and Pierce, 1975; Ehrlich, 1975). Most standards urge the primary analyst to justify at least the analysis and choice of the unit of analysis, provide evidence to rule out rival explanations, and the like. Often, these justifications are not uniformly agreed upon, so they may not be resolved as part of the prerelease critique. When alternative statistical models imply that the original results are invalid or misleading, additional steps must be taken to resolve the differences.

Secondary analysis—that is, reanalysis—of the primary evaluation is a partial solution to this problem. Moving beyond critique and criticism and the inherent problem of providing plausible alternative explanations of conjectures requires empirical assessment. Secondary analysis entails specifying and executing competing analyses and sometimes inclusion of additional evidence (Wortman, Reichardt, and St. Pierre, 1978). However, this is not always successful in resolving conflict (Boruch, Cordray, and Wortman, 1981), and in some cases, it may be necessary to seek other forms of conflict resolution (Boruch, 1981).

To facilitate the secondary analysis process, data from the primary study must be made available in usable form. All the standards that we reviewed acknowledge such requirements, but they are not explicit about what constitutes adequate documentation. The practitioner who attempts to accommodate Robbin's (1981) 140-plus technical guidelines for documenting data files may find that effort daunting.

Impending Issues

The standards-setting activities initiated by the Evaluation Research Society and other groups make a useful contribution in clearly identifying the sensible steps of the evaluation process. In this sense, they are a useful model by which we can tailor our efforts to devise the most appropriate evaluation for a particular setting and program.

It seems unlikely that such activities will improve the quality of practice (and reports stemming from evaluation efforts) in the absence of some quality control mechanisms. Two types of review procedures have been described in this chapter: prerelease critique (akin to an evaluation audit) and summative assessment of the extent to which conclusions follow from the evidence provided. Each type of review requires additional resources and careful monitoring of the costs and benefits.

Use of the review procedures assumes that the evaluation was properly specified at the outset. The cornerstone of all evaluation projects is the original set of questions to be addressed. According the the ERS Standards, these issues are to be formulated and negotiated at the outset. The ERS Standards are explicit in stating that the needs of the clients and decision makers are to be identified and addressed in the evaluation. Further, the information that is collected is to be justified by its usefulness and value for informing decision-makers or clients. These concerns are central if evaluations are to be used, and certainly they warrant careful attention. Rigorous tests of the extent to which an innovation exceeds standard practice may be seen as too time-consuming, as uninformative for short-term program decisions, or as requiring too long a wait between the time when the program is initiated and the time when data become available to answer the questions. This is all true, to a certain extent, and it is easy to make a rational case for avoiding these types of assessments. There is danger, however, in placing too much emphasis on the short-run informational needs of the immediate clients. The ERS Standards, as a package, leave the impression that client questions should take priority. If the client is not interested in high-quality impact assessments, we are left with the choice of performing the requested evaluation tasks or of not doing the evaluation at all. If the issue is to accumulate knowledge about how interventions influence social welfare, failing to promote rigorous tests of the effectiveness of social innovations would be a serious oversight in the long run.

Another element of the formulation and negotiation phase that causes this writer some concern is the need to avoid foreclosing options for creative exploitation of the situation in order to provide more sophisticated assessments. This requires a certain amount of flexibility, which translates into cost. Too much specification at the negotiation phase can foreclose these options.

79

Finally, the evaluation industry is diverse. Consequently, there are numerous views about the conduct of evaluations and the most feasible techniques (Boruch and Cordray, 1981; Bunda, 1981; House, 1981; Kennedy, 1981). However, the issue is less one of which method should be used but of how methods can be combined. The ERS Standards may facilitate this process, not so much for what they prescribe on a standard-by-standard basis as by virtue of their completeness. Multiple lines of evidence (Lipsey, Cordray, and Boruch, 1981) will have to be gathered in order to answer even a few of the issues raised. If this is true, in the future we should find more carefully documented evaluations focused on program process, outcome, and adequacy of the evaluation.

References

Anderson, J. K., Johnson, R. T., Fishbein, R. L., Stonehill, R. M., and Burns, J. C. *The U.S. Office of Education Models to Evaluate E.S.E.A. Title I: Experiences After One Year of Use.* Washington, D.C.: U.S. Office of Education, 1978.
Becker, H., and Kirkhart, K. "The Standards: Implications for Professional Licensure and Accreditation." *Evaluation News,* 1981, *2* (2), 153–156.
Bernstein, I. N., and Freeman, H. E. *Academic and Entrepreneurial Research: The Consequences of Diversity in Federal Evaluation Studies.* New York: Russell Sage Foundation, 1975.
Boruch, R. F. "How Can and Should Potentially Controversial Research Results Be Disclosed." Research paper, Department of Psychology, Northwestern University, 1981.
Boruch, R. F., and Cordray, D. S. (Eds.). *An Appraisal of Educational Program Evaluations: Federal, State, and Local Agencies.* Washington, D. C.: U.S. Department of Education, 1980.
Boruch, R. F., and Cordray, D. S. "Reactions to Criticism of the Holtzman Report." *Educational Researcher,* 1981, *10,* 10–12.
Boruch, R. F., Cordray, D. S., and Pion, G. M. "How Well Are Educational Evaluations Carried Out?" In L. Datta (Ed.), *Local, State, and Federal Evaluation.* Beverly Hills, Calif.: Sage, 1981.
Boruch, R. F., Cordray, D. S., Pion, G., and Leviton, L. "A Mandated Appraisal of Evaluation Practices: Digest of Recommendations to the Congress and the Department of Education." *Educational Researcher,* 1981, *10,* 10–13, 31.
Boruch, R. F., Cordray, D. S., and Wortman, P. M. "Secondary Analysis: Why, When, and How." In R. F. Boruch, P. M. Wortman, D. S. Cordray, and Associates, *Reanalyzing Program Evaluations: Policies and Practices for Secondary Analysis of Social and Educational Programs.* San Francisco: Jossey-Bass, 1981.
Bowers, W., and Pierce, G. "The Illusion of Deterrence in Isaac Ehrlich's Research on Capital Punishment." *Yale Law Journal,* 1975, *85,* 187–208.
Bunda, M. A. "Some Comments on the Recommendations in the Holtzman Project." *Educational Researcher,* 1981, *10,* 14.
Campbell, D. T., and Boruch, R. F. "Making the Case for Randomized Assignment to Treatments by Considering the Alternatives: Six Ways in Which Quasi-Experimental Evaluations in Compensatory Education Tend to Underestimate Effects." In C. A. Bennett and A. A. Lumsdaine (Eds.), *Evaluation and Experiment.* New York: Academic Press, 1975.

Campbell, D. T., and Erlebacher, A. E. "How Regression Artifacts in Quasi-Experimental Evaluations Can Mistakenly Make Compensatory Education Look Harmful." In J. Hellmuth (Ed.), *Disadvantaged Child, Vol. 3: Compensatory Education—A National Debate.* New York: Brunner/Mazel, 1970.

Chalk, R., Frankel, M. S., and Chafer, S. B. *AAAS Professional Ethics Project: Professional Ethics Activities in Scientific and Engineering Societies.* Washington, D. C.: American Association for the Advancement of Science, 1980.

Cook, T. D., and Gruder, C. L. "Metaevaluation Research." *Evaluation Quarterly,* 1978, *2,* (1), 5-51.

Cordray, D. S. "Standards for Judging the Impact of Social Programs." Paper presented at the annual meeting of the American Psychological Association, Los Angeles, 1981.

Cordray, D. S., Boruch, R. F., and Pion, G. M. "How Are Evaluations Carried Out?" In R. F. Boruch and D. S. Cordray (Eds.), *An Appraisal of Educational Program Evaluations: Federal, State, and Local Agencies.* Washington, D. C.: U.S. Department of Education, 1980.

Ehrlich, I. "Deterrence: Evidence and Inference." *Yale Law Journal,* 1975, *85,* 209-227.

Evaluation Research Society. *Standards for Program Evaluation.* Evaluation Research Society, 1981.

Evaluation Research Society. *Exposure Draft: Standards for Program Evaluation.* Potomac, Md.: Evaluation Research Society, 1980.

Gamel, N. N., Tallmadge, G. K., Wood, C. T., and Binkley, J. L. *State ESEA Title I Reports: Review and Analysis of Past Reports and Development of a Model Reporting System and Format.* Mountain View, Calif.: RMC Research Corporation, 1975.

Glass, G. V. "Integrating Findings: The Metaanalysis of Research." In L. Shulman (Ed.), *Review of Research in Education,* Vol. 5. Washington, D. C.: American Educational Research Association, 1978.

House, E. "Critique of the Northwestern Report." *ERS Newsletter,* 1981, *5,* (2), 8.

House, E. R., Glass, G. V., McLean, L. D., and Walker, D. "No Simple Answer: Critique of the Follow Through Evaluation." *Harvard Educational Review,* 1978, *48,* 128-160.

Joint Committee on Standards for Educational Evaluation. *Standards for Evaluations of Educational Programs, Projects, and Materials.* New York: McGraw-Hill, 1980.

Kennedy, M. "Assumptions and Estimates of Evaluation Utility." *Educational Researcher,* 1981, *10* (10), 6-9.

Lipsey, M. L., Cordray, D. S., and Berger, D. E. "Using Multiple Lines of Evidence in Evaluating a Juvenile Justice Program." *Evaluation Review,* 1981, *5,* 283-306.

Lyon, C., Doscher, L., McGranahan, P., and Williams, R. *Evaluation and School Districts. (Preliminary Report).* Los Angeles: Center for the Study of Evaluation, 1978.

Magidson, J. "Toward a Causal Model Approach for Preexisting Differences in Nonequivalent Control Group Situation: A General Alternative to ANCOVA." *Evaluation Quarterly,* 1977, *1,* 399-420.

Mosteller, F., Gilbert, J. P., and McPeek, B. "Reporting Standards and Research Strategies for Controlled Trials: Agenda for the Editors." *Controlled Clinical Trials,* 1980, *1,* 37-58.

Robbin, A. "Technical Guidelines for Documenting Machine-Readable Files." In R. F. Boruch, P. Wortman, D. S. Cordray, and Associates, *Reanalyzing Program Evaluations: Policies and Practices for Secondary Analysis of Social and Educational Programs.* San Francisco: Jossey-Bass, 1981.

Sechrest, L. "The Standards: A General Review." *Evaluation News,* 1981, *2* (2), 145-147.

Stake, R. E. "Setting Standards for Educational Evaluations." *Evaluation News,* 1981, *2* (2), 148-152.

U.S. General Accounting Office. *Assessing Social Program Impact Evaluations: A Checklist Approach.* Washington, D. C.: U.S. General Accounting Office, 1978.

Wargo, M. J., Tallmadge, G. K., Michaels, D. D., Lipe, D., and Morris, J. J. *ESEA Title I: A Reanalysis and Synthesis of Evaluation Data from Fiscal Year 1965 Through 1970.* Palo Alto, Calif.: American Institutes for Research, 1972.

Wortman, P. M., Reichardt, C. S., and St. Pierre, R. G. "The First Year of the Educational Voucher Demonstration: A Secondary Analysis of the Student Achievement Test Scores." *Evaluation Quarterly,* 1978, *2,* 193–214.

David S. Cordray is assistant professor of psychology and associate director of the Division of Methodology and Evaluation Research at Northwestern University. His research interests include evaluation policy, secondary analysis, and inference and judgment processes in applied social research.

Adoption of the Standards by ERS requires consideration of legal and
government implications of adopting codes of conduct in general
and the Standards in particular.

Legal and Government Implications of the ERS Standards for Program Evaluation

Jerry Cahn

As part of the ERS Standards Committee's process of developing the Standards, four subcommittees were formed to focus on relevant issues and to report on these issues to the Council to assist it in its considerations. This chapter reports the analysis of the subcommittee charged to address the legal and legislative implications of adopting the Standards.

The subcommittee focused on the potential legal implications for persons who refer to themselves as *evaluators* and for the ERS as an association. It also focused on the government implications for both parties. The scope of government, rather than legislative, implications was chosen because legislatures delegate authority to administrative agencies that perform the same activities that legislatures do, especially in relation to professions such as evaluation. For instance, the Ohio legislature has authorized its state department of mental health to perform oversight functions, and the department in turn has proposed standards for program evaluation by boards and contract agencies (Lyons, 1981).

This chapter is a revised version of the report of the ERS Standards Committee Subcommittee on Legal and Legislative Implications submitted to the ERS Council in October 1981.

P. Rossi (Ed.). *New Directions for Program Evaluation: Standards for Evaluation Practice*, no. 15. San Francisco: Jossey-Bass, September 1982.

The subcommittee also expanded the focus from the implications of the Standards per se to the implications of codes of conduct in general. There were two reasons for this expansion. First, the introduction to the Standards states that the ERS may consider other standards of performance in the future (for example, for personnel and product evaluation). The ERS Ethics Committee also is considering development of a code. Thus, it is already more efficient to discuss the range of issues that the ERS should consider when adopting codes of conduct in general than it is to focus merely on the Standards.

To understand the legal and government implications, one should understand four things: the legal and government duties and obligations of evaluators and the ERS in the absence of a code of conduct; the legal and government implications for evaluators and the ERS of adopting codes of conduct; the legal and government implications for evaluators and the ERS of adopting the present Standards; and the legal and government issues that the ERS should consider if it considers adopting additional codes of conduct.

Legal and Government Duties and Obligations of Evaluators

This is not the place to discuss in depth the legal rights and duties of evaluators. Therefore, the discussion here is designed only to point out issues of concern. When individuals engage in evaluation activities, they automatically subject themselves to the same duties, obligations, and potential liabilities that most researchers and consultants incur in their activities. These duties, obligations, and potential liabilities exist, whether an association or society adopts a code of conduct (for example, ethical or performance standards) or not and whether the association provides legal advice or not. The individual should be aware of these duties and obligations, and such issues should be separated from the implications of adopting codes. These issues include matters involving contracts, torts, statutes, and the Constitution.

Contractual issues of concern to evaluators include the following: When does a contract exist? What does the contract include? (For example, the Parol Evidence Rule excludes extrinsic—oral—matters.) What are the rights and duties of parties (especially third-party beneficiaries)? What issues affect termination of contract (for example, doctrines of impossibility, frustration, and substantial performance)?

Tortuous injuries include such issues as defamation of character, libel, slander, fraud, abuse, negligence, and the defenses available. At the present time, malpractice falls into the group of general tortuous issues, since no code of conduct for evaluators has been incorporated into federal or state laws.

Statutory and constitutional issues of concern to the evaluator include privacy, confidentiality of records, due process, rights to trial, restrictions on release of data, and informed-consent considerations. Also relevant are the

85

oversight rights posessed by various federal offices (for example, the Office of Management and Budget) to audit program that use public funds.

A government—either state or federal—can have an impact on evaluators in both of its roles: as a governing body that serves the public and as a contractor. The implications for government involve the following: the use of codes in certifying and licensing professionals, use of codes to assess the credibility of evaluators who provide testimony while conducting oversight investigations, and the use of codes by an administrative agency to license evaluation work performed for it by groups or individuals and to guide its investigations of evaluators' testimony and work products.

During the 1970s, governments, especially the federal government, became the primary funders and contractors of evalutions. Thus, sensitivity to the quality of evaluators' work products is a critcal issue: If government as contractor is dissatisfied with the work product, then government as regulator may use its licensing and related powers. It is not surprising to see government bodies, such as the Ohio state legislature, providing some general guidelines for its contracting agencies. If the agencies control the quality of evaluations, further intervention by the legislature is avoided.

The 1980s promise a change in the role of the federal government. Sensitivity to evaluations will focus not only on quality issues but also on the ability of evaluators to provide useful information for immediate policy decisions, many aimed at increasing the efficiency with which government funds are used. Increasingly, states will be directly involved with contracting evaluators, as funds for program operation shift to the states. Finally, efforts by the Reagan administration to motivate the private sector to become involved may increase the interest of the private sector in developing new evaluation tools. In sum, the federal government is less likely to be a direct contractor for evaluation, and in the context of the deregulation temper of the 1980s, government bodies are less likely to want to regulate evaluators' activities. However, as evaluators provide more services for other clients, regulation may be a role that state legislatures, administrative agencies, and private enterprise increasingly feel called upon to exercise.

If charged with malpractice, the evaluator's duty would be to show that all reasonable steps have been taken to adhere to the general standards of the profession, as evidenced by expert witnesses. (*Evaluation,* here, is considered to be a profession, as that term is defined by *Webster's* (1980, p. 911): "a calling requiring specialized knowledge and often long and intensive academic preparation." Indeed, in order to demonstrate that they took all reasonable steps in performance of their activities, evaluators should always include disclaimers in their reports concerning factors not available for measurement and use.

The situation concerning malpractice may change, regardless of the ERS's actions. Any client can adopt a general set of standards and demand that evaluators adhere to it as a condition of the contract. Similarly, any state legislature can decide to adopt its own standards and use them as criteria for certification and licensure and as standards that evaluators must follow when performing state contracts.

Legal and Government Duties and Obligations of the ERS

Even if it had no Standards, the ERS would have to recognize its legal and governmental obligations. If an evaluator is sued for malpractice, it is not unreasonable to expect the parties to seek ERS aid for identifying expert witnesses who can testify to the general standards of conduct for evaluators. Also, defendants can seek an amicus curiae (friend of the court) brief to support their position. The ERS should also expect federal and state legislatures and administrative agencies to call upon it to identify experts who can serve as witnesses at hearings that review evaluation studies as part of an oversight activity. The ERS may also be called upon by a government committee that is considering adoption of a code of conduct for evaluators.

Obviously, whether it adopts the Standards or any other code of conduct, the ERS has the right to honor or refuse such requests. The fact that the Joint Committee on Standards for Educational Evaluation has developed some standards (Joint Committee on Standards for Educational Evaluation, 1981) provides the ERS with additional flexibility. However, once the ERS adopts a code of conduct with some specificity, it should expect the number of such requests to increase, and it becomes obliged to honor them. The ERS should realize that it may be compelled to have representatives testify in court cases, since courts are likely to consider adherence to the Standards as best evidence of proper performance by evaluators.

Legal and Government Implications of Adopting a Code of Conduct

Typically, a society or association adopts a code of conduct in order to provide education and training to future professionals, provide guidance to professionals in their practice, provide guidance in accreditation or licensing of a group of professionals, and regulate the activities of professionals (Ridings, 1980).

Societies use different terms to indicate the purpose of their codes—*standards, guidelines,* and *principles.* While the use of these terms is not always precise and terms are used interchangeably, they have differing legal and governmental implications. For this reason, distinctions are important. *Webster's* defines the three terms as follows: A *standard* is something established as a rule or basis of comparison in measuring or judging capacity, quantity, content, extent, value, and so on (*Webster's,* 1980, p. 1125); a *guideline* is an indication or outline of policy or conduct (p. 506); while a *principle* is a comprehensive and fundamental law, doctrine, or assumption upon which others are based (p. 908).

By definition, guidelines are most likely to be used for educational, training, and guidance purposes, and, because of their lack of specificity, it is unlikely that they will have legal ramifications. Standards range in their level of specificity and in their use. The more specific they are, the more likely it is that they will be used for accreditation, licensing, or professional regulation. When they do have specificity and they are used for such purposes, they have legal implications for both the professional society and the individual professional. To simplify discussion, therefore, let us consider all standards as being either guidelines—lacking specificity and not designed for accreditation or professional regulation—or true standards, which have the specificity needed for comparisons and which are available for use in accreditation and regulation.

Antitrust Implications of Adopting Codes of Conduct

The major issue for societies or associations is whether they are engaging in unlawful antitrust actions when they offer codes of conduct for their members. The issue has become increasingly important, due to the expansion of the definition of *learned professions* over the years and to increased attention to the issue by the Federal Trade Commission.

Black's Law Dictionary (1968) defines *profession* as "a vocation, calling, occupation, or employment involving labor, skill, education, special knowledge, and compensation or profit, but the labor and skill is predominantly mental or intellectual rather than physical or manual (*Maryland Casualty Co. v. Crazy Water Co.,* Tex. Civ. App., 160 S.W.2d 102, 104). The method or means pursued by persons of technical or scientific training (*Board of Supervisors of Amherst County v. Boaz,* 176 Va. 126, 10 S.E.2d 498, 499). The term originally contemplated only theology, law, and medicine, but, as application of science and learning are extended to other departments of affairs, other vocations also receive the name, which implies professed attainments in special knowledge as distinguished from mere skill (*Aulen v. Triumph Explosive,* D.C. Md., 58 F Supp. 4, 8)" (p. 1375).

In *Appalachian Power Co. v. American Institute of Certified Public Accountants* (177 F. Supp. 345, S.D.N.Y. 1959, aff'd per curiam 268 F.2d 844 (2d Cir, 1959), cert denied, 361 U.S. 887 (1959)), the courts affirmed the right of societies to develop codes of behavior for members. The decision held that professional bodies had the right to accept the public obligation for the unfiltered expression of their views: "[I]n the absence of economic motives and with the existence of procedures adequate to avoid patent unfairness, collaborative standards are not subject to antitrust laws. . . . Courts may not dictate or control the procedures by which a private organization expresses its honestly held views."

In recent years, the antitrust issue has been raised again, when societies alleging to regulate professional conduct through standards and enforcement procedures have been accused of restraining trade through monopolistic practices. In *Goldfarb* v. *Virginia Bar Association* (421 U.S. 773 (1975)), the Supreme Court decided that the Sherman Antitrust Act (1890) did not exempt a county bar association from mandating a fee schedule, since this was an illegal conspiracy to fix prices. In *Virginia State Board of Pharmacy* v. *Virginia Citizens Consumer Council, Inc.* (425 U.S., 748 (1976)), the court held that a state statute prohibiting pharmacists from advertising prices of prescription drugs was unconstitutional as a violation of the First Amendment. In *Bates* v. *State Bar of Arizona* (433 U.S., 350 (1977)), the ban on advertising by lawyers imposed by the Arizona State Supreme Court was removed. Further, in the *National Society of Professional Engineers* v. *United States* (435 U.S. 679 (1979)), the court held that a professional canon of ethics prohibiting competitive bidding by engineers was per se a violation of the Sherman Act. Finally, it should be noted that association codes can be challenged even when they are not actively enforced by an association through disciplinary proceedings. In *American Medical Association* (FTC Docket No. 9064 (Oct. 12, 1979) 94 F.T.C. 701), the Appellate Court noted that unenforced association codes are objectionable if they have a "chilling effect" on the conduct of members and thus thereby restrain trade.

Recently, Pollard and Liebenluft (1981) reviewed the antitrust issues involved in professional societies' development of standards for the Federal Trade Commission. According to these authors, the major factors to consider in examining standard-setting initiatives are the following: First, does the standard setting limit the consumer choice? That is, to what extent does denial of membership as a result of standard setting exclude potential competitors, and are there less restrictive alternatives? Second, are the standards reasonable? Third, is operation of the program procedurally fair? That is, does it include procedural safeguards, such as notice of hearing and right of appeal when the organization intends to use the standards for certification, and does it impose sanctions for improper conduct?

In sum, the key questions from an antitrust viewpoint are whether the standards are reasonable and whether they restrict competition. As already noted, even voluntary and advisory codes are subject to antitrust scrutiny if they have a chilling effect on trade. When a professional society sets up procedures, due process is necessary. Due process includes the following procedures: written notice of the alleged violation, proposed sanction, and right to comment or hearing; a hearing on the matter, if requested, at which the member may present views, personally or through a representative, such as a lawyer; and the right to appeal an adverse decision to some higher authority, such as the association board of directors or another, impartial, governing board (Jacobs, 1981; Lunch, 1979; Rockwell, 1981).

Product Liability of Members of Standards Committees

The American National Standards Institute (ANSI) examined the legal liability of people who served on standards committees and of the organizations that sponsored such committees. The conclusions that ANSI drew (American National Standards Institute, 1975) are generally applicable to the liability of individuals working on any national consensus committee.

In a legal action, claims of product liability can turn on allegations based either on a theory of negligence or on strict liability. According to the ANSI counsel and to the search of this ERS subcommittee, no one has ever held a national voluntary standards organization liable under either the negligence doctrine or the strict liability doctrine. Nevertheless, it is useful to understand the potential grounds for liability, especially under negligence theory, which claimants are more likely to use.

To bring a successful claim against standards-committee members for negligence, a plaintiff would have to show three things: that they owed a duty of care to him, that they breached this duty, and that this breach was a proximate cause of the injury. In *Hall* v. *E. I. DuPont de Nemours and Co. Inc.* (345 F. Supp. 353 (E.D.N.Y., 1972)), the courts held that when individual members of an industry choose to delegate the function of safety investigation and design to the industry as a whole and its trade association, then liability for negligence can be placed on the industry as a whole. This decision implies that if the ERS assumes the responsibility for developing standards that specify detailed methodological procedures for evaluators to follow, it could be held liable for negligent design and application of the resulting Standards.

A second theory of negligence rests on the decision handed down in *Hanberry* v. *Hearst Corp.* (276 Cal. App. 2d680, 81 Cal. Rptr. 519, 39 ALR 3d 173 (1969))—negligent misrepresentation and reasonable reliance thereon. The issue raised in this suit was whether the Good Housekeeping Seal of Approval had been granted negligently to a hazardous product, with the Seal constituting "certification" of quality that misled a purchaser who eventually suffered an injury. The implication for the ERS is that it could be held liable for "certifying" quality evaluations that eventually injured their consumers.

The third and most likely negligence theory involves liability to third parties for negligent performance in development of standards. Based on the *Hempstead* v. *General Fire Extinguisher Corp.* approach (269 Supp. 109, D. Del. (1967)), the adoption of standards by voluntary standards committees could be held to constitute tacit approval of the safety level of products that meet those standards, particularly where it can be foreseen that evaluators will rely on the standards. The implication for ERS is that its Standards Committee has the burden of showing that it exercised reasonable care in developing the Standards to avoid risk of harm.

Assuming that an injury was caused to the client of an evaluator when the evaluator adhered to a standard that was deficient, and assuming that the duty of reasonable care was held to exist, the plaintiff must demonstrate that the members of the Standards Committee actually failed to use reasonable care. In determining whether reasonable care was used, two standards could be adopted by the court. First, if the individuals on the Committee have "in fact, knowledge, skill, or even intelligence superior to that of the ordinary man, the law will demand. . . conduct consistent with it" (Prosser, 1980, p. 161). Second, the standards of care will be measured at least partially against the "custom in the trade" and the opinions of experts in the field. The implication for ERS is that it must demonstrate a wide range of input from evaluators and use the best possible expertise in development of its Standards.

It should be noted that simple reliance on the expertise generally used by evaluators may not be enought. In *Marsh Wood Products* v. *Babcock and Wilcox Co.* (207 Wis. 209, 240 N.W. 392 (1932)), the defendant relied upon the consensus of industry and expert opinion, but the plaintiff's experts demonstrated that the consensus (for determining the safety of steel boiler tubes) was inadequate, given current technology. Thus, the obligation of the ERS is to demonstrate that both the best possible, and the latest, expertise were used in developing its Standards.

The doctrine of strict liability holds a manufacturer or seller liable for an injury caused by a defect in the product without requiring proof of fault or negligence on the part of the manufacturer or seller. The doctrine is usually used to allocate risk to the party best able to avoid harm and also to provide sellers with an incentive to reduce product hazards. This doctrine has not been used, and it is not likely that it will be used against national voluntary standards organizations, since they do not gain pecuniary advantage from use of the standards and they do not have the large resources necessary to lower product risks.

Legal and Government Implications
of Adopting Standards

As the ERS Standards state, the ERS was established in 1976 to serve the professional needs of people engaged in program evaluation. The Standards were developed because members of the ERS searched for a concordant set of principles or "standards to guide program evaluation practice and focus attention on issues facing the emerging profession." This indicates that the purpose of the Standards is for guidance and education.

An analysis of the Standards' content leads to a similar conclusion. For example, the Standards are general in nature and offer no specific measures for comparisons. While the document is admonitory in tone, with each standard phrased as a *should* rather than as a *can,* this does not render the nature of the actions to which evaluators may adhere any more specific. Further, the standards include no provisions of even a pseudolegal nature. They do not explicitly state to whom they apply, disciplinary actions that should be taken if someone violates a standard, or enforcement procedures that can be taken in the face of violations. Finally, the Standards are no more specific than the *Standards for Evaluations of Educational Programs, Projects, and Materials* (Joint Committee on Standards for Educational Evaluation, 1981), which have been judged to be so broadly written that individuals declaring themselves bound by them can hardly be held liable for failure to follow any one (Johnston, 1981).

Since the Standards actually take the form of guidelines, it is unlikely that the ERS Council, members of the committee that wrote the Standards, and evaluators who voluntarily adhere to them will be subject to new legal liabilities related to malpractice issues. The Standards also do not expose the ERS to antitrust liabilities. Since the Standards do not specify who belongs to the profession, they make no effort to monopolize the profession, and they do not produce an anticompetitive effect. Thus, it is unlikely that an evaluator who does not belong to the ERS will sue it for exclusion or that the Federal Trade Commission will assert a monopolistic or even a "chilling" effect on free trade by evaluators. Finally, it is unlikely that the Standards will produce a lawsuit related to the due-process issue so long as the ERS keeps a record demonstrating open input (including public notice to provide comments) in development of the Standards.

However, it is likely that the ERS will find itself subject to new legal and government responsibilities as a result of adopting the Standards. These responsibilities include the following: being called upon as an amicus curiae by evaluators who are being sued for malpractice; being called upon by plaintiffs in such cases to provide expert witnesses to attest to proper professional conduct (members of the Standards Committee are most likely to find themselves thus solicited); and being called by legislatures and administrative agencies that have an interest in developing or adopting standards for evaluators, whether for accreditation, licensing, or contract criteria purposes.

One recent case demonstrates the potential involvement of the ERS in a lawsuit. In *Forrest* v. *Ambach* (No. 7715–80, before the Supreme Court of the State of New York, County of Albany), a psychologist sued the Commissioner of Education after being fired allegedly "in retaliation for her thorough evaluation of children suspected of having handicapped conditions, which, petitioner says, tended to expose respondents' attempts to avoid their statutory obligations regarding such children." Forrest claimed that she followed the *Standards for Providers of Psychological Services* and *Ethical Standards for Psychologists* developed by the American Psychological Association (APA). Accordingly, the APA and its New York counterpart offered themselves as amici curiae on her behalf, stating that she had acted properly (Pallak, 1980). The actual court decision did not deal with the APA *Standards for Providers*. Instead, the court based its decision on the statutory rights of handicapped children and on the petitioner's right of free speech and expression, as guaranteed by the First Amendment. Thus, this court's decision suggests that, at this time, courts will tend to rely more on statutory and constitutional arguments than on adherence to voluntary standards developed by professional organizations.

The significant point for the ERS is the action of the APA. Since Forrest asserted that she had been fired for adhering to the *Standards for Providers of Psychological Services,* the APA decided to submit an amicus brief in support of the petitioner. It is likely that, should something similar befall an evaluator, the ERS would have to consider submitting an amicus brief in support of the petitioning evaluator.

Legal and Government Implications of Adopting the Present Standards

Adoption by the ERS of the present standards has three implications that evaluators should recognize, although they may not be realized for quite some time. Both stem from the precedent value of the ERS's having standards for performance of some evaluations. (It should be noted that these implications also apply to the Joint Committee's standards.)

First is the bandwagon effect. Once codes of conduct are developed by evaluators, it is likely that they will also be used by potential clients, including government bodies that may use them when drafting their own codes for evaluators. The Joint Committee developed one code; the ERS now develops a second. The General Accounting Office, the Office of Management and Budget, and other government agencies that perform evaluations may feel the need to develop codes of their own, especially if they are concerned about having evaluators take efficiency and accountability considerations into account. The advantage of adoption by the ERS of the Standards is that it may stem the tide of others' developing their own. At the least, it offers interested parties another authoritative source on which to rely.

Second, but less likely, is the possibility that courts will begin to hold evaluators liable to a higher standard of care than they now follow. As noted before, people usually are held to be liable for negligent behavior if they violate the "reasonable, ordinary, prudent person" standard. However, professionals are held to higher standards; they are expected to possess and exercise the knowledge and skills of a member of the profession in good standing. "A person who is a professional with special skills is required to possess and exercise the knowledge and skills of a member of the profession in good standing in the same or similar localities" (*Words and Phrases,* Vol. 34, p. 391). Thus, now that the ERS has adopted the Standards, evaluators can expect to be drawn into complex legal battles to determine what the standards of performance are and to determine whether the evaluator under fire used the appropriate level of skills and knowledge. (It is possible that this would occur even without the adoption of the Standards. Since a plaintiff is more likely to win if a defendant is held responsible for a higher standard of conduct and since many people consider evaluators to be professionals, any plaintiff is likely to follow this line of attack.)

A third potential implication for evaluators is posed by efforts either by the public or (more likely) by evaluators to translate the Standards into criteria for licensure. However, this is not a very likely event in the near future. The experiences of other professional groups indicate that a move for state licensing of evaluators would not be welcomed by state legislators. Indeed, such a step is seen as an an effort to control the number of people entering the profession, and it raises antitrust and monopoly considerations.

Legal and Government Implications of Adopting Additional Codes of Conduct

The introduction to the Standards states that the ERS was established to serve the professional needs of people engaged in program evaluation. The Standards Committee recognized that its document is "a live one, subject to periodic reexamination and revision." Also, the present Standards may be only the first of many sets of standards. Accordingly, the ERS should be aware of the general legal and government implications that development of more specific standards for program evaluation or other codes of conduct can have.

Purpose. The purpose of a set of standards is the essential first element in its design. There is a trade-off between the value of a code of conduct to regulate the activities of a profession and the legal and government implications that stem from it. As noted, the ERS Standards are so broadly written that neither the ERS nor an evaluator is likely to be held liable for damages if an evaluator is accused of malpractice and asserts adherence to the Standards. However, the absence of specificity in the Standards makes them ineffective in providing direction in concrete situations or in creating for the public the image of a profession that is willing to regulate itself.

What are the short- and long-term professional needs of evaluators? That is the first question that must be answered when considering the development of new codes. Second, what kind of commitment are evaluators and the ERS prepared to make to meet these needs? Are general sets of standards to be developed by a host of voluntary organizations (for example, the Joint Committee and the ERS) and by government bodies (for example, the Ohio Department of Health)? This leaves open the possibility that conflicting standards will be developed. As governments seek greater accountability among the evaluators who perform studies for them, they may feel the need to have evaluators adhere to certain codes of conduct. Are evaluators prepared to have governments or their support arms (which may be influenced by political concerns) fill the gap caused by the absence of professional standards, or are the evaluators willing to bite the bullet? What kinds of financial and time commitments are evaluators prepared to make to allow an organization like the ERS to regulate the profession? The next four paragraphs discuss some issues raised by these questions.

Membership. Who will be included in the group accountable for adhering to ERS codes of conduct? Will it be anyone who calls himself or herself an evaluator, or will some criterion be used to credential evaluators? Will criteria be informal, or will an effort be made to obtain state credentialing based on them? It would be an expensive enterprise to do so. Are evaluators prepared to invest in the machinery needed to guarantee members that the due-process procedures necessary to avoid potential lawsuits (for example, public notices, hearings, drafts, and files) are carried out?

Court Involvement. As already noted, if standards have some specificity, they offer best evidence in a court of law concerning appropriate practices for a profession. If the ERS adopts additional codes, the likelihood that evaluators will be involved if malpractice cases occur will increase, as will the likelihood that members of the Standards Committee will be called upon in such cases.

Enforcement Procedures. A number of enforcement and disciplinary procedures would be needed to enable the ERS to regulate itself. These include due-process procedures such as fair notice and hearings. The experiences of other professional organizations in this area are useful. Ridings (1980) reviewed the disciplinary and enforcement procedures used by a number of professional groups, especially by the auditing and accounting professions, and found that the attention paid to self-regulation by individual groups differs significantly. Analysis shows that punitive measures to enforce standards usually are not effective, because of the secrecy of disciplinary actions, the failure to address significant problems, and inaction due to litigation. The implication is that the willingness to confront the question of violation of standards may be more important for professional status than the ability to enforce such standards — or, at least, this is now true. This point is emphasized by the present reliance of the Security and Exchange Commission (SEC) on the American Institute for Certified Public Accountants's regulation of CPAs, although the SEC is authorized by law to regulate them. Auditors have also developed an impressive handbook describing their disciplinary procedures.

The cost of operating a disciplinary and enforcement structure must also be considered. The American Psychological Association enforces its *Ethical Standards* with a structure that costs $100,000 a year. As a result of this expense, APA has decided not to enforce its performance standards with a similar structure (Kilburg and Mills, 1981).

Conclusion

The analysis outlined in this chapter was performed to provide the ERS Council with a set of opinions concerning the legal and governmental implications of the Standards for Program Evaluation and to confront issues involved in the adoption of future standards. It is based on recent experiences that other associations and societies have had with their standards. Current legal cases could change the situation, and additional analyses should be performed before future codes of conduct are adopted.

The analysis indicates that no significant new legal and government liabilities can be expected to fall on the ERS or on evaluators as a result of the ERS's adoption of the Standards. However, the ERS should expect increasingly to be involved with legal and government issues as the Standards become widely known. As the ERS considers expanding these Standards and developing other codes of conduct, other issues will arise. While these issues may pose legal and government problems, the experiences of other societies indicate that the problems can be overcome.

References

American National Standards Institute. *Products Liability of Members of Standards-Writing Committees.* New York: American National Standards Institute, 1975.
AICPA Professional Standards. Chicago: Commerce Clearinghouse, 1976.
Black's Law Dictionary. (4th ed.) Minneapolis: West, 1968.
Jacobs, J. "Professional Codes of Ethics Have Anti-Trust Contexts." In *Association Letter.* Washington, D.C.: Chamber of Commerce, August 1981.
Johnston, J. Personal communcation to members of the ERS Standard Committee, January 16, 1981.
Joint Committee on Standards for Educational Evaluation. *Standards for Evaluations of Educational Programs, Projects, and Materials.* New York: McGraw-Hill, 1981.
Kilburg, R., and Mills, D. Personal communication, July 1981.
Lunch, M. "Do the Professionals Have a Future?" *Legislative Monitor,* 1979, *14* (9), 6–7; *14* (10), 10.
Lyons, R. Personal communication, 1981.
Pallak, M. Personal communication to American Psychological Association Board of Directors on amicus brief in *Forrest* v. *Ambach,* October 10, 1980.
Pollard, M., and Liebenluft, R. *Anti-Trust and the Health Professions.* Washington, D.C.: Office of Policy Planning, Federal Trade Commission, 1981.
Prosser, W. *The Law of Torts.* (4th ed.) Minneapolis: West, 1980.
Ridings, J. "Self-Regulation Through Standard Setting: Lessons from Accounting and Auditing." Paper presented at the annual meeting of the American Educational Research Association, Boston, 1980.

Rockwell, W. "Government Attack on Professional Organization." Paper presented at the Organization Management annual meeting, Washington, D.C., 1981.
Webster's New Collegiate Dictionary. Springfield, Mass.: Merriam, 1980.
West. *Words and Phrases.* Minneapolis: West, 1976.

Jerry Cahn, a psychologist and attorney who specializes in human service program and policy development, is a member of the standards and ethics committees of the Evaluation Research Society. He is a director of TAGOR Associates, a government relations firm, and IDEAS, a nonprofit consulting firm. Cahn is currently engaged in Garden City, New York, as the administrative director of Dental World Centers, Inc.

Index

A

Abt, C., 22
Abt, W. 22
Abt Associates, 37
Accreditation and licensing, and standards, 86, 87, 91, 93, 94
American Educational Research Association, 17, 29, 36
American Institute for Certified Public Accountants (AICPA), 94, 95
American Institutes for Research, 37
American Medical Association, and antitrust issue, 88
American National Standards Institute (ANSI), 89, 95
American Personnel and Guidance Association, 17
American Psychological Association (APA), 17, 18, 29, 36, 47, 48, 50, 51, 57, 92, 95
Amicus curiae, and standard setting, 86, 91–92
Anderson, J. K., 69, 79
Anderson, S. B., 2, 17, 19, 21–26
Antitrust, and codes of conduct, 87–89
Appalachian Power Co. v. American Institute of Certified Public Accountants, and antitrust issue, 87–88
Auditor General of Canada, 8, 17
Aulen v. Triumph Explosive, and antitrust issue, 87

B

Ball, S., 17
Barnow, B. S., 61, 65
Baron, J. B., 17, 22, 23, 26
Baron, R. M., 17, 22, 26
Bates v. State Bar of Arizona, and antitrust issue, 88
Becker, H., 69, 79
Berger, D. E., 79, 80
Berk, R. A., 4–5, 59–66
Bernstein, I. N., 77, 79
Binkley, J. L., 80
Board of Supervisors of Amherst County v. Boaz, and antitrust issue, 87

Boruch, R. F., 67, 68, 70, 74, 75, 76, 77, 79, 80
Bowers, W., 77, 79
Braskamp, L. A., 19, 23, 24
Bunda, M. A., 79
Burns, J. C., 79

C

Cahn, J., 5, 83–96
Campbell, D. T., 4, 54, 56, 57, 61, 64, 65, 75, 77, 79–80
Carter, L. F., 2, 3, 37–48
Chafer, S. B., 70, 73, 80
Chalk, R., 70, 73, 80
Chicago, University of, National Opinion Research Center at, 37
Codes of conduct: and antitrust issues, 87–89; legal implications of, 86–87, 93–95
Cohen, W. M., 19, 22
Coles, C., 22
Committee on Evaluation Research, 17
Communication and disclosure: and large organizations, 45–46; Standards on, 15–16; strengthening of, 34
Companies. *See* Research and evaluation companies
Comptroller General of the United States, 18
Construct validation, and Standards, 56–57
Context evaluation, 9
Contracts: and evaluators, 84; and Standards, 39–40
Cook, T. D., 54, 56, 57, 68, 77, 80
Cordray, D. S., 2, 67–81
Council for Applied Social Research (CASR), 7
Cronbach, L. J., 4–5, 49–58

D

Data analysis and interpretation: and large organizations, 44–45; Standards on, 15
Data collection and preparation: and large organizations, 44; Standards on, 14